MONTANA'S FLATHEAD COUNTRY

BY ROBERT C. (BERT) GILDART

NUMBER FOURTEEN

MONTANA GEOGRAPHIC SERIES

PUBLISHED BY

Montana Magazine, Inc.

HELENA, MONTANA

RICK GRAETZ, PUBLISHER
MARK THOMPSON, DIRECTOR OF PUBLICATIONS
BARBARA FIFER, ASSISTANT BOOK EDITOR
CAROLYN CUNNINGHAM, EDITOR—MONTANA MAGAZINE

This series intends to fill the need for in-depth information about Montana subjects. The geographic concept explores the historical color, the huge landscape and the resilient people of a single Montana subject area. All typesetting, design and layout production completed in Helena, Montana. Printed in Japan by DNP America, San Francisco.

ACKNOWLEDGMENTS

The author wishes to thank Jan Wassink, who helped with research and wrote parts of the sections on natural history and natural resources. The author also expresses his appreciation to Mike Engstrom of Achilles Raft Company for the use of rafts, to David Gildart for accompanying him through frothy whitewater, and to Mrs. Gildart, Sr., for allowing her husband to accompany the author through those turbulent sections where he brushed against the bottom of the Flathead River on more occasions than he might care to remember.

CONTENTS

The Author
Robert C. "Bert" Gildart is a free-lance writer/photographer with credits in many national and international publications. Assignments take him to Europe and over North America.

Photographs on these pages, clockwise from top left:
Flathead mist JAN WASSINK; *the Middle Fork* ROBERT GILDART; *the South Fork* ROBERT GILDART; *the Jocko River* GEORGE WUERTHNER; *bison roundup* WILLIAM A. MUNOZ; *Flathead Valley farm* LAWRENCE DODGE; *blue grouse* JAN WASSINK

PART I

FLATHEAD RIVER COUNTRY

WATERS OF THE FLATHEAD

The Fountainhead of the Flathead

Nature has graciously provided a method for replenishing the sparkling—and sometimes muddy—waters that flow through Flathead country. Beaming down warmly, the sun transforms the Pacific Ocean's frothy surfaces into water vapor. Each energized particle rises and soon begins to coalesce with others. In their aggregate, they form massive cloud formations that move inland—sometimes quickly and violently but, at other times, quite casually over long, lazy days marked by luminous clouds and inky-black shadows.

As they approach the mighty Rockies, these water-bearing clouds are compressed. The clouds ascend mountain masses along the backbone of the Rockies that rise to heights of more than 10,000'. The headwaters of the Flathead River System lie here.

As the clouds rise, they cool and their precipitation falls on the upper reaches of Flathead country—on Glacier National Park, and the Bob Marshall and Great Bear wilderness areas. In some locales, rain and snow provide between 80 and 100 inches of water annually.

Much of the rainwater and snowmelt percolates into the soil, emerging as a multitude of springs. In other sites, water from rain and melting snowbanks flows overland, forming tiny creeks that meander through alpine meadows. Only some of these streams assume the same path year after year and thus have been given names: Stretching across the upper reaches of Flathead country are Little Salmon, Kintla and Scalp creeks. As watercourses, they are minuscule. But soon, they gather with others and begin to grow—merging, intertwining, intermixing as gravity draws them downward. Eventually they become the North, South and Middle Forks of the Flathead River.

Moisture-laden clouds blown in from the Pacific are dispersed over Flathead country. JEFF GNASS

The Three Forks of the Flathead River

The three forks of the Flathead River receive most of their water between April and June. Warm weather, often coupled with periods of rain, initiates the surge of spring runoff. Stream levels can rise very rapidly from April through mid-May, and peak flows often exceed 10 times the average flow. During 1964, heavy rains on top of an above-normal snowpack brought record flows to the North and Middle Forks and the larger Flathead River, causing extensive flooding in the upper Flathead River Valley. Flows on the Middle Fork rose to nearly 50 times their annual average.

But that was unusual. Normal high flows generally provide excellent whitewater rafting for four to six weeks, with the runoff beginning to taper by mid-June. Streamflows drop steadily throughout summer as the high-elevation snowpack shrinks and the resultant groundwater flow into the tributaries lessens.

Water returns to the Pacific via rivulets, streams and the major forks of the Flathead.
Left: Middle Fork of the Flathead. LAWRENCE B. DODGE
Top: South Fork of the Flathead. ROBERT GILDART
Center: Confluence of the North Fork and the Middle Fork. TOM ULRICH
Bottom: Lower Flathead River. TOM DIETRICH

The three forks of the Flathead are widespread and drain vast areas. The North Fork of the Flathead River arises in southeastern British Columbia, where it is called the Flathead River. At the border, its name changes to the North Fork of the Flathead. Flowing south the river collects water: From Canada, it receives about 28 percent of its volume while along the 58-mile reach of the North Fork in the United States, the river draws water from at least 16 major tributaries, four of which drain large lakes in Glacier National Park.

The Middle Fork of the Flathead River originates at the northern end of the Bob Marshall Wilderness. It flows in a general northwesterly pattern through the Great Bear Wilderness. Below its junction with Bear Creek, the river follows most of the southern boundary of Glacier Park. Numerous tributaries feed the river from both sides. One of these, McDonald Creek, drains the 6,800-acre Lake McDonald in Glacier National Park.

The South Fork of the Flathead River originates at the southeast end of the Bob Marshall Wilderness and runs through the heart of it before entering 39-mile-long Hungry Horse Reservoir formed by 564-foot-high Hungry Horse Dam. The North, South, and Middle Forks contribute more than 90 percent of the upper Flathead River's flow; the Stillwater and Whitefish rivers are the most important tributaries downstream from the point where the three northern forks merge. The annual flow into the upper Flathead River—before it enters the Flathead Lake—averages 7.6 million acre-feet. The Swan River contributes another 880,000 acre-feet of water directly to Flathead Lake at Bigfork.

Left: The Flathead River has lofty origins in areas such as Upper Kintla Lake in Glacier National Park. LAWRENCE B. DODGE
Above: In spring the Swan Range and Swan River provide a considerable volume of water that empties into Flathead Lake near Bigfork. TOM DIETRICH

Flathead Lake

With a full-pool surface area of 197 square miles, a maximum length of 27 miles (the local and presumably correct measurement) and a maximum width of 15 miles, Flathead Lake encompasses the largest area of any natural freshwater lake in the western United States. Residential dwellings speckle much of the 161-mile perimeter, while undeveloped shoreline sections are dominated by coniferous forests, rock outcrops and gravel beaches. The Mission Mountains provide the scenic backdrop to the east side of the lake, forests dominate the northwest shoreline, and rolling grasslands back the southwest corner.

Both Tally Lake and Lake McDonald in the Flathead Basin attain greater maximum depths than Flathead Lake's 370 feet. Flathead can be divided into four distinct regions based on depth characteristics. The shallow delta is located at the mouth of the Flathead River at the extreme north end of the lake. There, the deposition of sand and other materials during spring runoff has built up the lake bed, and depths are generally less than 20 feet. A relatively level shelf exists on the west half

Above: Lake McDonald in Glacier National Park.
GEORGE WUERTHNER
Right: Flathead Lake near Polson. TOM DIETRICH
Far right: McDonald River in Glacier National Park.
TOM DIETRICH

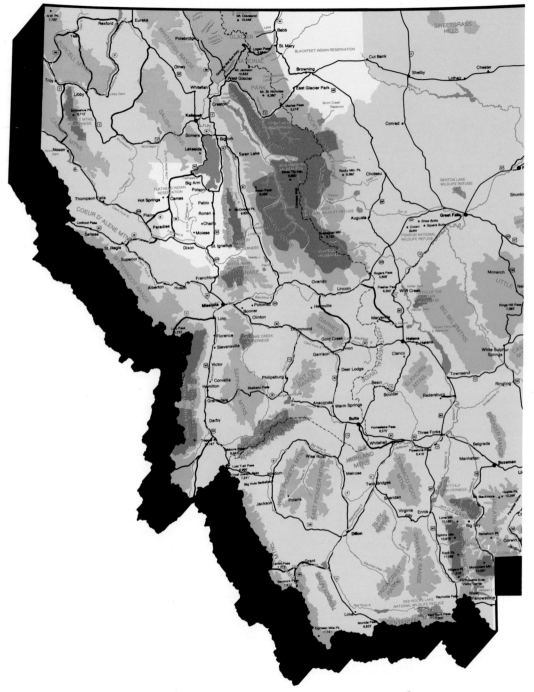

of Flathead lake. This region, which begins just beyond the steep shoreline dropoff, ranges in depth from 80 to 150 feet. A deep trough reaching depths greater than 300 feet underlies the entire eastern half of the lake. Polson Bay, at the southern end of Flathead Lake, is isolated from the main body of the lake by an island-dotted strait called the Narrows. Polson Bay is generally less than 25 feet deep and constitutes the most extensive shallow area of the lake.

The aquatic environment of Flathead Lake is strongly influenced by inflowing waters from the Flathead and Swan Rivers. Natural events and human activities throughout the upper Flathead drainage add sediments, nutrients, ionization and organic matter to the rivers, and most of these elements are ultimately discharged into the lake. This riverine inflow plays a profound role in shaping the water quality and biological communities of Flathead Lake.

Flathead Lake collects water from a 4.5-million-acre drainage, encompassing the upper Flathead River system, the Swan River, and small stream watersheds emptying directly into the lake. The lake discharges into the lower Flathead River at Polson.

The Flathead River annually discharges 7.6 million acre-feet of water into Flathead Lake, while the Swan River adds another 880,000 acre-feet. The considerable influence that these rivers exert on Flathead Lake can best be understood in light of the relative volumes of the lake and river waters. During an average year, Flathead Lake receives a yearly inflow of 8.8 million acre-feet of water, most of which comes from the major river tributaries. The lake volume is 18.8 million acre-feet, or about 2.1 times greater than the annual inflow. In other words, almost half of the lake volume is replaced by river water each year.

This replacement rate is rapid for a large lake. In contrast, water in Nevada's Lake Tahoe has a residence time estimated at 700 years, reflecting its extreme depth (more than six times that of Flathead), large volume and the lack of a major river inflow and outflow.

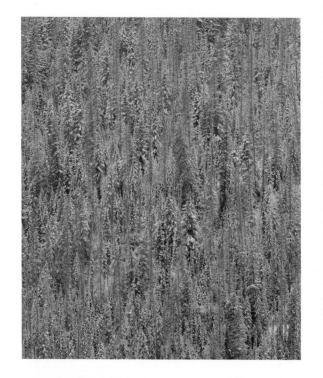

The Lower River

After circulating through the lake, the waters from the high ground of Flathead country exit the lake from the southwest side of Polson Bay. The bay has a large surface area and averages only about 16' in depth, giving the sun ample opportunity to warm the waters before they exit the lake via the old river channel and Kerr Dam. The highest water temperatures in the river system occur just below Kerr Dam. Maximum water temperatures at Columbia Falls measure around 68 degrees, maximum water temperatures just below the dam may rise to more than 74 degrees. After passing through Kerr Dam, the waters once again resume their southward course as a river.

Called by some the "Forgotten Flathead," the lower Flathead River stretches almost 70 miles between the dam and its confluence with the Clark Fork River near Paradise. Relatively inaccessible to the public, these 70 miles

Left top: March snowfall on the South Fork. JEFF GNASS
Left bottom: The old steel bridge at Kalispell. KRISTI DuBOIS
Above: Flathead River between Paradise and Perma. LAWRENCE B. DODGE

have only four public access points, at Buffalo, Sloan's Bridge, Dixon and Perma. The lower Flathead River drains 156,358 acres and is a low-gradient river. As it meanders south and west, the main river picks up the water from four tributaries: the Little Bitterroot River, the Jocko River, Mission Creek and Crow Creek. At its mouth, the lower Flathead has an annual discharge of 259.5 cubic yards per second, making it one of the largest rivers in Montana.

FORMATION OF FLATHEAD LAKE

According to today's geological theories, the features of the Flathead Valley were conceived eons before the vast Rocky Mountains appeared and streams began to flow.

The story of the lake begins almost 600 million years ago, in the Precambrian era, when a series of vast inland seas consecutively covered most of what is now North America. As these seas receded, they left a residue that hardened into rocks with the passage of time. These rocks would one day contribute substantially to the formation of Flathead Lake. But before that time, almost 600 million years would have to pass, while Mother Nature painted her portrait of the area.

One of the scenes in her slowly evolving picture was the brushing in of the Rocky Mountains. This was about 100 million years ago. From deep within the mantle of the earth, tremendous pressure built against the earth's crust, which broke into a number of huge blocks called

Left: Sailboats near Big Arm on Flathead Lake. RAY MILLER

Above: Flathead River's abundant sloughs indicate that the river is an old one. KRISTI DuBOIS

Many moons ago, raging waters flooded the Flathead Valley, drowning nearly all but a few of the chief's tribe. As the survivors fled to higher ground, the waters followed them.

Finally, all the land was covered except for one peak where a small band of Indians huddled. The chief said, "I will try to stop the water." And he asked his guardian spirit to help him.

He then shot an arrow toward the ground at the edge of the water. It barely missed the shore and floated away, as did a second. The third arrow stayed in the ground at the very edge of the waves. The water rose to the feathers, but went no higher. Gradually, much of the water receded, exposing the mountains, hills and valleys. The water that remained formed Flathead Lake.

Flathead Tribal Legend

plates. When these plates collided, their rise and fall formed hills and mountains. Thus one mountain chain, the remnants of which are known as the Rocky Mountains, began to rise some 55 million years ago. These were not the Rockies as we know them today. These ancient peaks were relatively devoid of vegetation, for, at the time, North America was a dry area. Few streams flowed, and those that did may be presumed to have been dull, lifeless ones lacking the wild surge that would later challenge whitewater adventurers.

In the geological sense, the dry period lasted no longer than the blink of an eye, a mere 60 million years. Termination of the period ushered in the last great geological epoch, the Pleistocene, a period 2 million years ago during which rain began to fall, mighty streams began to emerge, and ice was formed.

Tens of thousands of years ago, a glacier in the far north moved down the Rocky Mountain Trench through Canada. So vast was the glacier that, when it arrived in present-day Montana, a tongue crossed over the Continental Divide in Glacier Park and moved out upon the plains. Where the city of Kalispell is located today, the depth of ice is thought to have been 3,000 feet. To the east, the glacier covered portions of both the Swan and Mission Mountain ranges. The effects of the ice can be seen today, particularly in areas where these mountains are more rounded.

But the most significant local influence of the glacier would be its development of Flathead Lake. To do this, the mass of ice needed to scour out a basin that would hold a large quantity of water, and create a dam that would impound the water.

For a massive glacier, scouring out a basin must have been an easy job. As it moved constantly, its huge weight dug into the soft earth left by the inland seas. Simultaneously, at its sides and at its front, the glacier left great piles of earth and rocks called moraines.

Moraines in the Flathead Valley are of two different types. *Lateral* moraines, which formed along the sides of glaciers, can be seen to-

Above: The Mission Mountains tower majestically over the lower portion of the Flathead. CHARLES E. KAY

Left: Polson reposes atop the terminal moraine that contributed to the formation of the lake. ALAN CAREY

11

FLATHEAD LAKE'S SPRINGTIME "PLUME"

The turbidity plume is visible in this aerial view of Flathead Lake, looking toward the mouth of the Flathead River. JAN WASSINK

Although distinguished by its surface size compared to other lakes in the United States, Flathead Lake is relatively shallow, reaching a maximum depth of 370 feet, but averaging only 165 feet.

A highly visible "plume" in the lake, prominent only in the spring, is the river's water as it enters the lake. Because the river has gathered sediment upstream, its predictable discharge pattern in the Flathead Lake can be followed for weeks as it flows from north to south.

River waters warmed by air in their downstream course resist mixing with cold, dense lake water. The result is a narrow layer of light river water sliding across the surface of the lake. This readily visible, sediment-laden flow is termed the spring "turbidity plume," and provides a dramatic illustration of the Coriolis force. This phenomenon of the earth's rotation is the deflection of moving objects to the right, counterclockwise in the northern hemisphere (but to the left in the southern). The turbidity plume in Flathead Lake thus travels westward, toward Somers.

After reaching the west shore, the river waters continue their counterclockwise course and begin to head south. During this southerly passage, the plume generally hugs the western shoreline, taking about three weeks to travel from Caroline Point in the north to the Narrows above Polson Bay in the south.

From the air, the lake at this stage can present a striking view, with the west side appearing murky and tan and the east side remaining clear and blue. Westerly storms and resulting wave action, however, sometimes blur the sharp dividing line by spreading sediment-laden waters across the lake to the east.

The plume divides upon reaching the Narrows. One branch continues southward and spreads into Polson Bay, while the other branch heads east toward Finley Point. This latter branch of the turbidity plume completes its counterclockwise journey by heading north along the east shore. Woods Bay and the mid-lake regions are among the last waters to receive recognizable spring run-off sediments.

Plume visibility usually lasts about a month, from the entry of the main runoff flow in late April and early May, to early June. The surface waters clear within another two to three weeks, and the fine clay and silt settle through the entire water column of the lake in six to eight weeks.

day as low rolling hills flanking the Flathead Lake. *Terminal* moraines formed when the climate warmed enough to melt the front of the ice mass at a rate that maintained its "snout" in a relatively fixed position.

In the Flathead Valley, two terminal moraines were left as the climate stabilized. One of these lies north of Dixon and marks the place where the leading edge of the ice stood long enough for the great mass of earth—gravel, sand, clay and boulders—to accumulate from the melting ice. The surface expression of this moraine is a series of "pot holes" left by large blocks of melting ice. Today these watering holes attract an abundance of wildlife.

The other terminal moraine, the Polson Moraine, was instrumental in the creation of Flathead Lake. Originally, Flathead Lake was impounded by that moraine, a giant dam across the southern valley. Lake water overflowed the top of the moraine and promptly began cutting downward, creating a gorge and forming the southern extension of the Flathead River. This cutting action would have emptied the lake, or lowered its level, had the river not encountered the hard rock created from the sediments of the vast inland seas 300 million years previously. This rock prevented rapid drainage of the lake.

Today, Flathead Lake, now about 12,000 years old, occupies the trough scooped out by a great glacier and held in check by hard Precambrian rock. The deepest portions are just a short distance off the lake's east shore. But even this area may one day be filled. The silted plume of the Flathead River has caused a large delta to form in the north end of the lake. Given enough time, that delta could fill the entire lake.

Glacial Impact on Flathead Country

While the massive ice sheet spread south down the Rocky Mountain Trench, another ice sheet was moving down the Purcell Trench of northern Idaho. This ice mass stretched as far south as Coeur d'Alene, and its presence also would affect the Flathead Lake area.

Not far below the lower Flathead River, the ice dam slid across that current extension of the river, the Clark Fork, and quickly backed up both rivers to Missoula and beyond. The backwater covered the present-day site of Drummond, as well as that of Darby in the Bitterroot Valley, Ovando in the Blackfoot Valley and Hot Springs in the Little Bitterroot Valley.

Near Ronan these rising waters were 1,100 feet deep; they were 2,000 feet deep at the ice dam that made Red Sleep Mountain of the National Bison Range an island. Distinctive beaches developed on the Moiese Hills near Charlo. The "fingerprints" of these beaches can be seen from the lower portion of the Flathead River Valley as distinctive horizontal terraces on the surrounding hillsides.

University of Montana geologist J.T. Pardee was the first to recognize the signs of this prehistoric lake, which he named Glacial Lake Missoula. Eventually other geologists discovered the remains of similar, even larger lakes: Glacial Lake Spokane, Glacial Lake Great Falls and many others.

In the 1920s, Bretz, another geologist, became fascinated by signs of an enormous flood that had ravaged eastern Washington. The upper Grand Coulee had been ripped out of raw lava, there were dry waterfalls that had never seen a river, and thousands of channels had scoured away the rich volcanic soil and left only "The Scablands" of Washington state. These features generated a theory slowly accepted by the scientific community.

But little wonder the theory needed time to be digested. Bretz contended that Glacial Lake Missoula had breached its ice dam at least 35 times—thundering down the Clark Fork Valley and roaring across eastern Washington, releasing 9.5 cubic miles of water an hour. As outdoor writer Rick Hull of the Kalispell *Daily Interlake* noted in 1986, "it was as if Lake Michigan drained in two days."

Today, the most persistent features recording the effect on areas adjacent to the Flathead River are found in Camas Prairie just south of Hot Springs. When the ice dam broke, a wall of

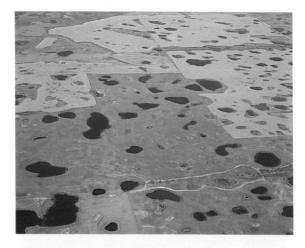

In their wakes, retreating glaciers left potholes and soil that is excellent for luxuriant stands of cherry trees. TOP: ALAN CAREY; BOTTOM: LAWRENCE B. DODGE

water 750 feet high spilled over the low divide that separates the Little Bitterroot River and Camas Prairie. Its legacy exists as ripples of gravel 25 feet high, extending for miles across the prairie.

While Glacial Lake Missoula was merging with waters of Glacial Lake Flathead, a finger of ice finally built its own moraine in the area west of Elmo, plugging up the interlake gap. Simultaneously the glacier shoved itself against Hog Heaven Ridge and other mountains, creating "kame terraces" where the slopes slumped on the glacier. These terraces, still visible high on the mountainsides at 4,300 feet above sea level, show the tremendous depth of the ice. Most significantly, however, the ice blocked the flow of the Flathead River and diverted it to the west, up the area called the Big Draw. Today, the Hot Springs road follows this draw. Numerous Pleistocene stream beds are still plainly visible on the gravel surface in the Big Draw. Geologist and Professor Lex Blood enjoys pointing out that the highway department has carefully installed culverts where the road crosses the ancient channels—"presumably in preparation for the next ice age."

But at last, the climate began to warm and, as it did, even more water followed the course of the Big Draw, merging in the area of present-day Dixon with the great body of water in Glacial Lake Missoula. With yet more melting, all ice receded and at last the river came to assume its present course.

Many other features of the lake region have been sculpted by the Flathead's last glacier. Visitors traveling up the west shore of Flathead Lake should look for Wildhorse Island, almost directly east of the town of Elmo. The rocky hills on Wildhorse Island were scoured by flowing glacial ice, resulting in a distinctly streamlined appearance: their northern sides slope gently, while their southern sides are extremely steep.

Other indicators of the glacier's presence are evident throughout the valley and are known as "erratics." Erratics are rocks left behind as huge chunks of ice melted.

Finally, the road between Polson and Bigfork winds through apple and cherry orchards on the east shore of Flathead Lake, many of which are growing on rich soils deposited during the glacial age that ended 10,000 years ago.

WILDLIFE AND WILDFLOWERS

Flathead Country's Basic Wealth

Surrounded by glacier-carved peaks reaching upward to 10,000 feet, the area of the Flathead drainage is one blessed with an unusual diversity of spectacular natural beauty and unparalleled natural resources. The native people, white explorers, fur traders and settlers were lured here by the bountiful wildlife and lush vegetation. Today, visitors are lured here by these same features.

Within the drainage of the Flathead ecosystem lie a part or all of a national park, three state parks, four wilderness areas, a national forest, three state forests, four national wildlife refuges, four state waterfowl production areas, 11 state recreation areas and 18 fishing access points. And, of course, the largest natural freshwater lake west of the Mississippi, along with more than a hundred smaller lakes.

The diverse habitat is home for nearly half of the grizzly bears in the contiguous 48 states. The largest concentration of bald eagles known to these 48 states is found here as well as one of the densest nesting populations of osprey found anywhere in the world.

Another endangered species, the gray wolf, has once again moved into the drainage and may be on the comeback. Although not yet documented, one or more pairs of peregrine falcons are believed to be nesting in the south end of the drainage. And, despite the effects of man's intrusion into the environment, the fisheries contain an assortment of species that lure the most avid sportsmen.

Clockwise from top right:
Wolf. ALAN CAREY
Peregrine falcon, rarely photographed in the wild, is show here on a falconer's stand. CRAIG E. SHARPE
Grizzly bear. ALAN CAREY
Bald eagle. ALAN CAREY

Fisheries

Long before the first white man walked into the Flathead River Basin almost 200 years ago, westslope cutthroat, bull trout and mountain whitefish were the dominant fish in the system. Since then, slowly at first but moving more quickly as time went on, changes have been occurring in the valley. Logging, grazing and farming changed the character of the natural vegetation. These practices, coupled with mining, settlements and water diversion, altered the quality of the water moving through the system. With the completion of the Kerr and Hungry Horse dams, the seasonal flow levels of the river was changed.

These changes altered the habitat of the native fish species, making it unable to support the numbers that once lived here. At the same time, almost everyone's favorite fish was dumped into the lakes and rivers to see how it would do. Some of these species, better able to handle the altered water conditions than the native species, have proliferated until they have become dominant in particular habitats in the basin.

Today, except for limited areas in the remote upper reaches of some tributaries, the fishery scarcely resembles that of the early 1900s. Although good numbers of westslope and bull trout still inhabit the waters in and above Flathead Lake, they share those waters with kokanee salmon and lake trout, rainbow trout and brook trout. Below Flathead Lake the northern pike has become the most important sport fish. With the exception of two lakes containing pure-strain westslope, the native westslope and bull trout populations have diminished to the point that they are almost nonexistent below Kerr Dam.

In spite of some of the dramatic changes that have occurred in the system over the last 75 years, Flathead fishing is still among the best in the state.

Top: Bald eagle, airborne kokanee fisherman at McDonald Creek. Not native to the area are salmon and northern pike, which have been the object of considerable study. MIKE LOGAN PHOTOS

became established in McDonald Creek in Glacier National Park. The first fishing season was authorized in 1933, and enthusiastic sportsmen took 100 tons of kokanee from Flathead Lake—approximately 200,000 fish.

The kokanee is a landlocked form of the Pacific sockeye salmon. After hatching in the upper reaches of freshwater rivers, sockeye salmon move downriver to the ocean to mature. In Flathead country, the lake provides a suitable substitute for the ocean.

In September, kokanee that have spent four years feeding in Flathead Lake begin schooling up in the north end of the lake, near where the Flathead River enters. Periodically, schools of these 13- to 17-inch fish begin moving up the river. Once on their way, they stop eating. As they move upstream their body chemistry begins to change and their normal silver color changes to copper or bright red. In addition, the males develop hooked jaws and humped backs. Once they reach the area where they had hatched four years previously, the females sweep out nests in the gravel, called redds, and deposit their 1,000 or so eggs apiece while the males fertilize them. Their life's purpose fulfilled, the adults die, providing food for bald eagles, mergansers, grizzly bears and other scavengers.

Kokanee

It is ironic that in an area of such abundant and diverse natural resources, the most sought-after fish is an introduced species. Kokanee salmon, introduced in the early 1900s, make up over 90 percent of the fish caught in the Flathead country each year. The Montana Department of Fish, Wildlife and Parks estimates that sportsmen spend more than $3 million in Flathead County on fishing tackle to pursue the kokanee. Add in the cost of gas, food, lodging and other related spending, and the figure climbs to more than $10 million—a significant amount in anyone's book.

Kokanee were first documented in the Flathead in 1918 in Lake Mary Ronan. They are believed to have come in with a shipment of chinook salmon eggs from Oregon. The following year, mature kokanee were found in Flathead Lake.

By the 1930s, kokanee had established themselves in the Flathead river system. Thousands of kokanee were spawning along the east and west shores of Flathead Lake and heavy spawing runs were going up the Flathead River and the Swan River. To the chagrin of then park officials, an early-season run of kokanee

Northern Pike

The Flathead River system is one of the few places in the west where northern pike can be found in a river environment. They have been introduced into many lakes in the drainage and now have access to almost the entire river system. It is in the Lower Flathead, below the lake, that they are most at home and have become the sport fish most highly sought by fishermen along that section of the river. They were first collected in the river system in the Little Bitterroot River in 1961. It is thought that fish from Sherburne Lake in Glacier National Park were introduced into Lonepine Reservoir during the fall of 1953. From there, they made their way into the river system.

16

Birds

The Flathead Valley, situated between the Mission and Cabinet Mountains about 3,000 feet above sea level, has a wide variety of habitats. Bird watchers looking forward to a day in the field could choose an exhilarating walk above timberline in pursuit of ptarmigan, horned lark, rosy finches and water pipits. Or, perhaps a less lofty walk through the montane forest, searching for Swainson's thrush, varied thrush, pine siskin or evening grosbeak. On the other hand, it could be productive to walk along a river bottom and listen to ruffed grouse drumming, great horned owls hooting and yellow warblers trilling. Birders would also enjoy a picnic by one of the many lakes or reservoirs to spot loons, goldeneye, mergansers, mallards and Canada geese.

Waterfowl are abundant, raptors common, and songbirds myriad. The Flathead hosts as many as 200,000 waterfowl, 600 bald eagles and 2,000 tundra swans on their various migrations, in addition to numerous other migrating species.

Clockwise from top left: Ruffed grouse drumming. TOM ULRICH
Great horned owl. JAN WASSINK
Wood duck. TIM CHRISTIE
Great blue heron. TIM CHRISTIE
Male yellow-rumped warbler. TOM ULRICH

The Flathead River between Kalispell and Flathead Lake supports one of the highest nesting densities of osprey in the world. Osprey using this nest, found along the road between Somers and Bigfork, have entertained passers-by for several years. TOP: ALAN CAREY; ABOVE AND RIGHT: JAN WASSINK

Osprey

In an article entitled "Final Call for Montana's Finest Fisherman," published in the March 1973 issue of *Montana Outdoors,* Doug and Don MacCarter, who had been studying the Flathead Lake osprey since 1966, wrote:

"In recent years, the Flathead Lake osprey have experienced a marked population decrease. Our study indicated organochlorine insecticides that affect the thickness of the eggshell and the egg's hatching ability may be responsible for the decline. Based on our studies, we have grave doubts about the future of the osprey.

"...more than one young per breeding female is necessary to maintain a stable osprey population in New York and New Jersey. If Flathead Lake ospreys are subject to similar mortality schedules, the Montana population is declining at a rate of three to four percent each year."

In the July 28, 1974 *Missoulian,* Jane MacCarter wrote an article entitled "Ospreys Hold Their Own at Flathead." In it, the good news was that "we've since found that the ospreys are managing to keep their population stable everywhere on the lake..."

Five years later, on July 18, 1979, the *Ronan Pioneer* ran an article entitled "Flathead Osprey Are Not Declining." The good news at that time, according to Bob Klaver, a Bureau of Indian Affairs biologist, was that the osprey seemed to be recovering, although it was still unclear why the birds were coming back.

The reason still is unclear but coming back they are! In 1966, the MacCarters located 16 occupied nests. By 1970, that number had grown to 25. By the time Bob Klaver and other tribe biologists picked up the osprey study in 1977, 38 pairs were engaged in raising young. In 1985, biologists located and mapped more than 100 active nests.

Osprey are found near most of the lakes and larger rivers in the drainage but the largest concentration of the birds, more than one third of the entire population, is found on the Flathead River between Kalispell and Flathead Lake. That section of river, roughly 22

miles long, meanders slowly through an already filled portion of Flathead Lake. During the 8,000 to 10,000 years of its existence, the Flathead River has been depositing silt in the north end of the lake. The low gradient through the delta resulted in the river's twisting and turning as it cut a path to the lake. Consequently, this section of the river is heavily braided—split into several channels, dotted with islands, bordered by numerous marshes and guarded by old oxbows reminiscent of a time when the river was even more uncertain of its destination than it is today.

This configuration of the river provides abundant habitat for many varieties of fish, and, in turn, food for the osprey. Many suitable nest trees, in the form of old snags, also can be found along this section of river. Whatever the reason, abundant food or a wide choice of nest sites, osprey are attracted to the area in large enough numbers to lead biologists to suspect that we are currently hosting one of the highest nesting densities of osprey anywhere in the world. And, as yet, there are no signs of the trend's reversing itself.

Based on the returns of several bands that had been placed on birds here in the valley, Flathead osprey are believed to spend their winters along the west coast of Mexico. They return to the Flathead about the middle of April.

Although the mates probably do not spend their winters together, they rejoin each other at the site of last year's nest. After rejuvenating the nest by adding a few fresh sticks, the female lays from one to four eggs. Incubation takes about four weeks. The newly hatched young are immediately introduced to the food they will eat all of their lives, fish.

To hunt, the birds soar and hover over the water, searching for any unwary fish that may wander too close to the surface. When one is spotted, the osprey dives, feet first. If the aim is true, the talons drive into the fish, the osprey thrashes free of the water and returns to the nest to feed the young. By the last of July, the young have fledged. Even though they can fly freely and often go great distances from the nest, the newly fledged birds still return to the nest at night to roost. By the end of September, they have already headed for warmer climes.

The Canada goose is the valley's most prominent species of waterfowl. The species is troubled by a shortage of safe nesting sites, however. Artificial nesting structures may increase reproductive success in the future. JAN WASSINK PHOTOS

Geese

When geese were first studied in the Flathead, they nested primarily on islands, muskrat lodges and other similar sites at or near the highwater mark of the river. Since the building of Kerr and Hungry Horse dams, the situation has changed. During maximum discharge, some of those nests are flooded out, resulting in nesting failure. During minimum flows, waters drop enough to expose land bridges between the islands and the mainland. Predators use these bridges readily.

In the last few years, more and more Canada geese confiscated osprey nests for their own use. Since geese begin nesting in March, a full month before the osprey return from Mexico, the geese face no opposition when selecting the nests of their choice. When the osprey return to find a goose in their nest, a dispute may occur.

The rapidly increasing osprey population may provide badly needed nest sites for the geese and thus spur the Canada goose population at the same time. Another means of increasing the number of safe nest sites is through the use of nesting platforms. Tribe biologists have found that 84 percent of the nests in artificial nest structures hatched young while only 26 percent of the nests located on the ground survived to the birds' hatching stage.

Bald Eagle

Attracted by more than 125,000 kokanee salmon, which make their way to McDonald Creek in Glacier National Park, bald eagles have become a spectacle there that is heralded across the nation. During the height of the season, more than 3,000 visitors may travel to Glacier National Park to view the eagles from Apgar bridge. Totals for the season may run as high as 50,000 people.

Things were not always as they are today. The base of the phenomenon, the kokanee, was not introduced into the Flathead system until 1916. Before that time, bald eagles drifted through the Flathead on their way south from their breeding grounds in Canada and the Pacific northwest. But, with nothing to tempt them to stay, they paused for perhaps a day or two before continuing on their way.

After the kokanee established a spawning run in McDonald Creek in the mid-1930s, the large numbers of dead and dying salmon began attracting small numbers of eagles. In 1939, when the first records were kept, rangers reported 37 bald eagles along the creek. Numbers of salmon and eagles in the creek have increased steadily since then. The record high occurred in late November of 1981, when 639 eagles were counted.

The eagles arrive at the creek each day about 30 minutes before sunrise. As soon as it is light enough to see, feeding begins. Adult eagles may swoop down from their perches and pluck salmon directly from the surface of the water. Immature eagles often harass successful adults, attempting to steal their catches. This they try to accomplish through a series of aerial maneuvers and determined dives at the perching birds. Failing that, they may wade through the shallows to retrieve dead or stranded salmon.

After feeding for a couple of hours, the birds select a favored perch in one of the large trees along the banks of the creek. Bathing, preening,

The possibility of seeing several hundred bald eagles in a single day attracts almost 50,000 viewers each fall to Apgar Bridge in Glacier National Park.
KRISTI DuBOIS PHOTOS

resting and fishing continue throughout the rest of the day. Neither gregarious nor pugnacious, up to 30 eagles have been seen sharing the same tree.

By day's end, each eagle may have eaten as many as six salmon. In 1979 this represented a daily capture of more than 5,000 fish from the stream. Shortly before sunset, the eagles begin to leave the creek and fly to one of the roosting sites about two miles away.

21

More than 50 species of mammals occur in the Flathead. They include the bobcat, bison and black bear. LEFT: TIM CHRISTIE; TOP: WILLIAM MUNOZ; ABOVE: MIKE LOGAN

Mammals

Flathead country is just as abundantly blessed with mammals as it is with fish and fowl. From mountain goats, bighorn sheep, hoary marmots and pikas on the mountaintops, to white-tailed deer, otter and beaver in and along, the rivers, this country has them all.

Big game are especially numerous. Huntable populations of mule deer, white-tailed deer, moose, elk, mountain goats and bighorn sheep entice thousands of hopeful hunters to don fluorescent orange and take to the timbered slopes and river bottoms each fall. Bison and pronghorn, although they cannot be hunted, can be seen easily at the National Bison Range near Moiese. The woodland caribou, once common in lichen-covered old-growth forests throughout Flathead country, were extirpated primarily through logging of those mature forests. Although sightings are reported occasionally, a 1985-86 study found no evidence of the presence of these animals.

Like the caribou, lynxes, wolverines, fishers, otters and grizzly bears also require vast acreages of largely primitive land. While these animals are decreasing throughout their range in the contiguous 48 states because of loss of habitat, they are still relatively common here because of the broad expanses of land that exist largely unaltered.

Smaller mammals also are abundant. Columbia ground squirrels, red squirrels, deer mice, meadow voles, shrews and bats can all be found here, along with skunks, weasels, coyotes, red foxes, bobcats and badgers.

Wolves

Far up the North Fork, close to the Canadian border, a species is making history. Eliminated from the Flathead drainage more than 30 years ago, the wolf is on the comeback. Over the years, wolf sightings have been a regular, but infrequent, occurrence.

In 1978, a black wolf was frequenting the area of the North Fork just north of the border. Traps, set in hopes of capturing and radio-collaring this animal, captured a gray female instead. She was radio-collared and named Kishneena. Researchers for the Wolf Ecology Project tracked Kishneena until July 1980, when her collar stopped transmitting.

Continued monitoring of the North Fork area revealed the tracks of only a single wolf—until February of 1982, when ranger Jerry DeSanto spotted the tracks of two wolves traveling together in the northwest corner of Glacier National Park. One set of tracks was left by a female in heat and the other by a three-toed male. Later that year, numerous people reported seeing seven wolf puppies (three black and four gray) in an area just north of the border. In June 1982, the father of that litter, or another black three-toed male, was killed near the den site.

The excitement soon waned. A lone gray male, sighted along the North Fork, was the only wolf seen during 1983.

The summer of 1984 breathed new life into the Wolf Ecology Project. Reports of a female and six pups in the same area as the 1982 litter prompted a new effort at trapping and putting

Gray wolf. ALAN CAREY

radios on the wolves. In August, a male, dubbed Sage, was trapped and radio-collared. Wolf Ecology Project researchers followed the signals from his collar south, across the border into Glacier National Park. Finding the area to his liking, he spent the winter there.

In May 1985, bear researchers, working north of the border, inadvertently snared a lactating female wolf. Radio-collared and named Phylliss, she has become the hope of the future. A month after being collared, she was spotted from the air with seven all-black pups. Three of those pups were later captured and radio-collared. Because collars put onto pups must be loose enough to allow for growth, two of the pups were able to slip their collars, while a third pup, now named Kay, still wears hers.

By December 1985, the pack had taken up residence on the U.S. side of the border in Glacier National Park, just east of the North Fork between Camas Creek and McGee Meadows. Researchers have obtained good counts of the pack on several occasions. They believe the 12-member pack is made up of seven pups of the year, the breeding male and female, and three other adults. Dubbed the "Magic Pack," because

of the way it just magically appeared, the wolves have set up a home range of 250 to 300 square miles—a large territory for wolves. Researchers believe the large home range is a result of having no competition from neighboring packs. Although the only other wolf known to inhabit the North Fork area is Sage, the male collared in 1984, researchers believe there may be 15 to 17 wolves in the North Fork.

The wolves have found one of the major wintering areas for big game in the North Fork drainage and have centered their activities around that area. By tracking the animals as often as possible and checking kills, researchers have found that deer are the wolves' staple. Elk are also frequently taken and moose occasionally. The pack takes an average of a deer a day, or an equivalent amount of elk or moose.

Because of the abundant prey base, researchers aren't surprised that the wolves have returned. They are somewhat surprised that it took so long for them to reappear.

April 17, 1986, opened another chapter in the wolf recovery story. On that date, Phylliss, the breeding female of the pack, was located in Glacier National Park, just east of the interior

road going up the North Fork. Subsequent radio tracking over the next several months showed her staying close to that area, indicating to the researchers that she established a den there. Although it had not yet been confirmed by sight, researcher Mike Fairchild said, "If we know anything about wolves, there is a den there." The den was successful, making it the site of the first litter of wolf pups raised in Flathead country since early in this century.

With the addition of these new pups to the pack, researchers will be watching carefully for signs of the pack's splitting up. The 12-member pack was already larger than the usual average of six to eight animals. In addition, the 12 animals were cleaning up their kills so well that the researchers were having difficulties determining what the wolves had killed. Often, the only sign of a kill was a few blood stains in the snow. The addition of any pups would make a split almost imperative. There simply would not be enough food for each member.

It is also possible that the pack may have split before the breeding season. In that case, there could very likely be two litters. That chain of events could almost double the number of wolves in the North Fork in one year.

The spring of 1986 saw the capture of a third female. Trapped across the border in British Columbia, she subsequently returned to Phylliss's den site. The addition of a third radio-collared member of the pack will make the job of monitoring pack activities that much easier.

What is the future of the wolves in this area? Some folks, like ranger Jerry DeSanto, who has jurisdiction over the area currently being used by the wolves, believe they may just disappear—simply return to their former range in Canada. The wolf researchers believe that, with more animals and thus more possibilities for breeding, there is potential for rapid growth, and eventually dispersal. Meanwhile, the situation still is precarious at best. With all the eggs in one basket, one unforeseen incident could wipe out the entire population.

Flowers

Skunk Cabbage. At the first sign of spring, before the first hint of green leaves has even appeared, the bright yellow flower of the skunk cabbage appears, accompanied by the pungent odor for which it is named. If eaten raw, crystals of calcium oxalate in the plant produce a stinging sensation in the mouth that is not soon forgotten. The Indians learned to ignore the odor and found that roasting and drying eliminated the stinging, leaving a starchy root that made excellent flour.

Nodding Onion. The nodding umbel of this plant appears in Flathead country about mid-June. It was used by the Indians for flavoring much as cultivated onions are used today. Nodding onion is also consumed extensively by bears, ground squirrels, elk and deer.

Wild Hyacinth. From April to July, the edible corm of the wild hyacinth can often be found in large numbers in Flathead country. The corm can be eaten either raw or cooked. Boiling brings out its nutlike flavor, making it one of the tastiest of the native bulbs.

Sego Lily. The single white blossom and fragile-looking stem bely the presence of the delicious bulb found at its base. About the size of a walnut, the bulb is sweet and nutritious whether eaten raw or cooked. Boiling brings out a flavor resembling potatoes. As with the root of the skunk cabbage, the Indians ground it into a starchy meal which they then used for bread.

Glacier Lily. Early April often brings out myriads of these yellow flowers, which provide early spring nutrition for black bears, grizzly bears, rodents, deer, elk, bighorn sheep and mountain goats. The Indians used the leaves for greens, boiled the seed pods for a string bean, and either boiled and ate the bulb, or dried it for use in the winter.

Yellow Fritillary. This early spring flower first appears in March. Its single blossom is easily overlooked, leading to its Latin name meaning bashful. First appearing as a yellow-orange flower, it gradually turns to red as it

Clockwise from top right: Sego lily, glacier lily (ROBERT GILDART PHOTOS), *nodding onion, skunk cabbage* (JAN WASSINK PHOTOS)

25

Above: wakerobin. Top: clematis. Center: yellow fritillary. JAN WASSINK PHOTOS
Right top: bitterroot. Right bottom: wild strawberry. ROBERT GILDART PHOTOS

matures. Its starchy corm has a potato-like flavor when eaten raw and a rice-like flavor when cooked. Bears, Columbian ground squirrels and pocket gophers competed with the Indians for this early spring plant.

Wakerobin. Another early spring flower, the wakerobin or trillium is a welcome sight after the long winters in Flathead country. In addition to occasionally cooking the plant for greens, the Indians used the thick rootstalks during childbirth, which led to the name Birthroot.

Bitterroot. Beginning during the later part of April and continuing into July, this conspicuous pinkish flower can be found on many dry rocky sites throughout Flathead country. Although the blooming plant appears to be leafless, numerous leaves appear soon after snow melt, usually withering before the flower appears. Indians learned to locate the fleshy roots in early spring by the leaves. Since the stored starch has not yet been utilized by the developing flower, the root is tender and nutritious. Dug in large quantities, the white fleshy core can be baked, boiled or ground into meal. As its name implies, the root is bitter, a characteristic that disappears when the root is cooked. Used extensively by the Indians and the mountain men, and made famous in the journals of Lewis and Clark, the bitterroot is the Montana state flower.

Clematis. This lavender blue flower is the part of a slender, semi-woody vine that may grow to ten or twelve feet in length. Although it was not a food plant, early outdoorsmen quickly learned that the feathery styles that carry the seeds make excellent tinder. In addition, clematis was chewed by Indians and early settlers to relieve colds and sore throats.

Strawberry. Small and easily overlooked, wild strawberries have always been sought by man and beast. The berries are eaten by grouse, robins, rodents, bears and numerous other species of wildlife. In addition to eating the berries, early Indians stewed the leaves into a tasty tea-like beverage.

Rose. One of the most conspicuous and abundant flowering shrubs in Flathead country, the wild rose was an important winter food for the early inhabitants of the area. The rose hips

26

were eaten raw or cooked and made into jelly. Long after the fruit of most of the other trees and shrubs has dropped to the ground, the hips persist on the plant and are available when no other fruit can be found. This characteristic made them an important winter food for the Indians and early settlers and continue to make them important to many species of wildlife.

Yampa. Late in the season, from June to the end of August, yampa blooms. One of the best wild plant foods in Flathead country, raw yampa has a parsnip flavor. Cooked, it is sweet and mealy. The fleshy roots were collected by the Indians for food and also for trade. Shaped like small sweet potatoes, the tubers should be washed and scraped before boiling. They can also be dried and stored to be ground into flour as needed.

Kinnikinnick. Highly sought after by wildlife, kinnikinnick was probably used by the Indians in more ways than any other plant in Flathead country. They used the leaves as an extender for tobacco. The leaves can be used as an astringent, tonic or a diuretic. They contain tannin, which was used to cure pelts. The berries, when eaten off the plant in winter, have a bittersweet flavor that puckers the mouth. Boiling makes them sweeter and suitable for emergency food. Early settlers and Indians with cravings for tobacco packed their pipes with tobacco blend made from equal parts dried kinnikinnick leaves and dry inner bark of Red-osier Dogwood.

Arrowleaf Balsamroot. From the latter part of April into the first part of July, hillsides in Flathead country are tinted with the golden yellow of the balsamroot. The Indians used portions of the plant at all stages of its growth: They ate the young tender sprouts, the roots and the seeds. This plant is sought out by elk, deer and big-horn sheep.

Salsify. The large seed heads, which resemble giant dandelion seed heads, are much more conspicuous than the yellow flower itself. Introduced from Europe, salsify spread rapidly and was soon added to the list of plants used by the Indians for food. They also chewed its coagulated juice as a remedy for indigestion.

Left top: Indian pipes. JAN WASSINK
Left bottom: Wild rose. JAN WASSINK
Center: Arrowleaf balsamroot. ROBERT GILDART
Right top: Buttercups. BRUCE SELYEM
Right bottom: Wild hyacinth. JAN WASSINK

PART II

PEOPLING THE VALLEY

HISTORY

A First Christmas

On the 24th of December, 1813, a group of explorers and trappers were celebrating their first Christmas in Montana at the junction of the Clark Fork (formerly the Missoula River) and the Flathead River. At the time, a young man by the name of Cox was attempting to enjoy the day, but because of the atrocities being perpetrated on a Blackfeet warrior by members of the Flathead tribe, his day was less than joyous. In recounting his experiences, Mr. Cox wrote: "We spent a comparatively happy Christmas by the side of a blazing fire in a warm room...There was, however, in the midst of our festivities a great drawback from the pleasure we should otherwise have enjoyed. I allude to the unfortunate Blackfeet who had been captured by the Flatheads..."

Wendell Stephens, whose farm extends to the very spot where this episode occurred, can recite almost verbatim the passage quoting Cox in Peter Ronan's book *Historical Sketch of the Flathead Indian Nation.* Stephens and his wife are similar to many other Montanans who have worked the land all their lives. Their interest in the area is keen, and they have amassed a most intriguing collection of Indian artifacts and books that cover the early days.

"The horrible beating and maiming of the prisoner," says Stephens, "took place on a corner of my farm only a few feet from the river. At the time there were trees and a fort called the McMillan Trading Post. That 'first' Christmas took place just a few years after the first white people had come to Montana. First there was Lewis and Clark, but not far behind them was a man named David Thompson..."

At that point the afternoon for Stephens and me was cast. We talked until the light of day began to fade over this lower section of the Flathead River.

Snow-capped peaks and flower-strewn moraines flank St. Ignatius. JOHN KREMPEL

Famous Settlers

Development of northwestern Montana by whites came late in the history of the state, largely because of the geographical isolation of this region. North-south ranges of the Rocky Mountains presented a major barrier to migration into such sections as the Flathead Valley. The Lewis and Clark expedition, which began in 1804, overcame these obstacles. Eight years after Lewis and Clark returned to St. Louis in 1806, their journals were published, beginning to inform whites about this vast new land.

But intensive exploration—particularly in the northwestern portion of the state—was needed before widespread settlement would occur. British and American fur traders were the first explorers of the Flathead country.

David Thompson, the first white man to see the Flathead Indian country, was sent in 1808 by his employers, Canada's North West Company, to explore the area and to establish trade with the Indians. Having established posts west of Calgary the previous year, he and his party descended the Kootenai River into Montana. Thompson's lieutenant, "Big Finan" McDonald, established the first trading post where the town of Libby now stands.

Jocko Finley, a man of Scottish and Indian extraction, assisted David Thompson in 1809 by helping build the Kullyspell house on Pend d'Oreille Lake in what would be Idaho. He served as an interpreter and clerk on Thompson's first trip to the Mission Valley.

In 1809, David Thompson returned to the territory after wintering at Kootenay House in Canada, and built another trading post, the Saleesh House, located near the present town of Thompson Falls. He ranged far and wide, trading beads, jewelry, tobacco and other merchandise for pelts. Thompson's fair dealing so impressed the Flathead Indians that they offered friendship as well as fur pelts. Making a trading trip to their main camp, near present-day Dixon, Thompson first learned of Flathead Lake—called the Salish by the Indians—and the surrounding country. When he showed an interest in seeing the lake, the Indians provided a guide and horses. Then on February 29, he recounted that he "Engaged a Guide—the Gauche—& 2 Horses from Chief for a Journey the Morrow, please Heaven, to see the Saleesh Lake, & country around it."

On March 1, he headed north. "A fine day, but very sharp Night & Morng—Northly Wind....We came smartly on trot & hard Gallop to 1:25 p.m.—When we alighted on the top of Bare Knowl, commanding a very extensive View of the Lake and Country far around... Sketched off the Lake & c...at 3 p.m. we set off and held on very smartly, stopped abt 1/4 Mile to eat a mouthful at the wooded Brook...at 9 p.m. arrived, thank Heaven, at our Tents—all well."

Thompson described the lake as four to five miles by 20; but he obviously had seen only Polson Bay, with much of the lake hidden behind the islands at the lake's "narrows."

Although David Thompson left the Flathead Lake region in 1812, Finley, his trusted lieutenant, went into the southern part of the current reservation area at a later date. There, he too traded quite successfully with the Indians of the region and was in charge of the Spokane House, another fur trading post, until his death in May 1828. One of his grandsons, Piol Finley, was a very shrewd Indian who delighted in horse-trading with the whites in the Polson area around the turn of the 20th century. Finley Point, located northeast of Polson, was named for Piol, who lived there.

Jocko Finley's name stills echoes in the geography of the area. His first name was alternately spelled Jaco, Jacco, Jaccot, Jacquot, and Jocko. It is this last spelling that gave the valley, the river and the mountain range their present names. Many descendants live here.

In the winter of 1828-1829, Thomas Fitzpatrick, David Jackson, Joshua Pilcher and about 40 other traders and trappers stayed at Flathead Lake. Perhaps they were seeking a season's respite from the weather as well as from encounters with the war-like plains Indians over the Great Divide.

Angus McDonald. COURTESY ARCHIVES, UNIVERSITY OF MONTANA LIBRARY

Another man who contributed to white settlement and development here was Angus McDonald. Born in Scotland in 1816, he emigrated to America in 1838, where he entered the employ of the Hudson's Bay Company. Well educated, the man always traveled with a copy of Shakespeare's complete works in his knapsack. He fancied himself a playwright and poet, and in retirement, wrote extensively.

Like most traders in the area, he married an Indian woman. But unlike many others who abandoned their Indian spouses when they retired to Montreal or Toronto, McDonald stayed with Catherine and their 13 children.

The name Angus McDonald was soon known far and wide in the Indian territory; his reputation was similar to Thompson's. He was fair in his trading and he was trusted by Indians and whites. McDonald and Neil McArthur

Angus McDonald's grave (name spelling is unexplained) and remains of Fort Connah recall 19th century events in the Flathead. ROBERT GILDART PHOTOS

constructed Fort Connah (pronounced cone-naw) in 1846-47, and McDonald was soon put in charge. It was located approximately six miles north of St. Ignatius. Of the 18 original buildings, one is still standing.

What was Fort Connah really like? For one thing it was small. There were three or four log cabins, a bastion for defense measuring 14 feet square, a garden and a corral. At most, there may have been a dozen resident families. An accurate painting by Peter Tofft, now hanging in the Museum of Fine Arts in Boston, shows four buildings, a pile of winter firewood taller than a man, and four tipis scattered around the meadow.

As Rick Hull wrote in the Kalispell *Weekly News,* "To those expecting sharpened log walls and corner blockhouses the small log cabin is a disappointment, for the 'Fort' in Fort Connah is a misnomer. But at the same time, this abandoned trading post on Highway 93 between Ronan and St. Ignatius is a footnote to 50 years of history that turned the west upside down before the plow ever broke Montana soil."

From accounts of similar posts, a picture of life at the fort can be reconstructed. There was an icehouse for meat. While jerky was constantly being dried on racks, Indian women gathered the roots, berries or fruit in season. Sunday was set aside for rest and the wearing of Sabbath clothes. The surrounding Indian encampment would be the center of social life, immersing the trader in its family squabbles and in the rumors of Blackfeet aggression.

Boredom was the major enemy, and the trader might travel a hundred miles south to borrow books from Major Owen at Stevensville. Or he might do as Angus had done and find excitement in tribal ceremonies. But at least the fort was spared the long, cold winters of other northern posts. The huge Flathead Lake moderated the weather.

This post dealt mostly in buffalo goods. The Flathead Indians had been reluctant to trap beaver since it was a solo occupation, making them vulnerable to Blackfeet raiders and taking time away from food gathering. But they were happy to trade off the surplus buffalo goods from their annual hunts. In return for buffalo robes, pelts and meat, as well as saddles, rawhide rope, venison and dogs, the Flatheads received trade goods ranging from awls, thimbles and files to knives, fishhooks and guns.

During the 19 years Angus McDonald was in charge of Fort Connah, his business thrived. In 1864, he was promoted by the fur company to general supervisor of the various trading posts in the region. His son, Duncan, took over the business dealings at Fort Connah and guided the post successfully. But a number of forces were at work, from changing styles in clothing, to the discovery of gold in southwestern Montana, which helped bring an end to the fabulous fur-trading era. Fort Connah, the last operating fur post in the territory, was forced to close in 1871.

Angus McDonald retired to the Mission Valley and the tribes of the Flathead Reservation granted him the Fort Connah site, where he ranched until his death in 1889. His name lives on. Ten-thousand-foot McDonald's Peak overlooks the fort's remains, and a small lake reposes at its base. Upslope is a glacier that bears his name. Angus McDonald's son further helped perpetuate the name. Once, on a trip for supplies in Canada, Duncan camped at Apgar for an evening and carved his name on a tree. Although the tree has long since fallen, Lake McDonald in Glacier National Park would become a tribute to the MacDonald family. The old traders' descendants remain in the area. Joe McDonald was serving admirably as the president of the Salish-Kootenai Community College in 1986. His family still prizes the bagpipes Angus brought from Scotland.

Early Transportation

Early transportation in the Flathead Valley was very difficult due to a lack of roads in the mountainous terrain. Before 1885 all traffic through the valley was by wagon. To reach the country north of Flathead Lake in 1887, travelers and settlers took the Northern Pacific Railway spur to Ravalli. From there, they proceeded by wagon or stage as far north as the south shore of Flathead Lake. In 1888 Charles Allard, Sr., started a mail and passenger stage line from Ravalli to Lambert's Landing, later to be named Polson.

In 1889, Allard initiated another passenger and mail run to Station Creek on the southeast shore of Flathead Lake. A 14-passenger Concord stage was added in 1908, and Joe Allard, stopping only once to change horses at the Crow Creek station, could make the trip from Ravalli to Polson in good weather in about six hours.

From the north, passengers could take the main line of the Great Northern to Columbia Falls as early as 1905. They could then transfer to a spur line connecting south to Kalispell and Somers. Then, all that detained summer-time travelers from continuing either north from Polson, or south, was that picturesque body of water that stretched 30 miles long and spread 10 miles wide. To pass around Flathead Lake was difficult, although many did so—lured by necessity, or by the beauty of the newly discovered country.

Left: White Earth Creek, a spot mentioned in David Thompson's journals. RAY MILLER
Above: Remains of the steamboat Helena. ROBERT GILDART

Steamboats

Jack Kehoe, who lives at Holt, near the mouth of Flathead River, is well acquainted with the problem of travel in the lake in the latter part of the 19th century. From his living room window he can look out on his front yard and see the hull of the *Helena,* one of the last freight steamers on Flathead Lake. He has reason to be proud of the boat named for Montana's capital, because it was his father who built and captained it during the later years of lake transportation.

For a quarter century, starting in 1885, steamboats chugged on Flathead Lake from Demersville to the docks at Polson and back again.

The first Flathead freighter, the *Swan,* built in 1833 by Fred Lingle and Neal and George Nelson, had not been steam-powered, but rather equipped with a sail. This proved quite unsuccessful: the boat was caught in a dead calm that lasted three days and the crew was forced to row to shore.

In 1885 the boat was rebuilt, and a steam engine installed. The *Swan* was renamed the *U.S. Grant.* It was powered by steam from a small upright boiler, a "donkey engine" and a screw-type propeller. The captain was James Kerr, a former Great Lakes navigator.

The success of the *U.S. Grant* led to the construction of others, including the steamboat *Crescent.* The *Crescent* did a large business carrying people and freight from the southern port, Polson, to the northern terminus of Demersville. The steamboat even went on occasional Sunday excursions, which included picnics.

The *Crescent* was the first of the bigger boats with spacious freight decks, private cabins for passengers and well appointed dining saloons with adjacent galleys. Construction of the boat cost an estimated $16,000. Under favorable conditions the boat made the voyage from Polson to Demersville in three hours.

One passenger, David R. McGinnis, wrote of his August 9, 1890, experiences aboard the *Crescent:* "Our boat was crowded and freight was spread over everywhere and she was a small boat, but sturdy withal; nevertheless, we were somewhat uneasy to be embarked upon such a

Stoner's Landing, Flathead Lake Mont.

NEW KLONDIKE AT SAFETY ISLAND FLATHEAD LAKE MONT.

small craft, where long stringers of burning wood were constantly being discharged upon the decks and cargo, until it appeared to us that the boat would catch on fire and burn, and then, I thought, where will we be, far from shore and in water too deep for wading.

"But while I was anxiously watching those logs and fiery sparks, the other passengers were entirely unconcerned, playing scat and sledge all the way."

On November 20, 1890, the *Crescent* had trouble with ice, and its sides were severely ripped. Iron sides were subsequently attached to prevent future damage.

The lake cruiser, *State of Montana*, also flourished on Flathead Lake. Although built to navigate the Flathead River to Columbia Falls, the boat could do so only when the river was at flood stage.

At 130 feet long and with a 50-foot beam, the *State of Montana* was larger and faster than the *Crescent*. A three-decker with 16 staterooms, the *Montana* was propelled by twin engines and cost about $25,000. In a trial trip from the foot of the lake a few days before the Fourth of July in 1891, it carried 300 people. Later the boat broke loose from the dock during a storm and drifted downstream where it broke up on a sandbar at Foy's Bend.

Another boat, the *Pocahontas*, was built in the east and shipped to Montana on two large flatcars on the Northern Pacific Railway. In 1887 the *Pocahontas* ran aground in a storm. Burdened with 40 tons of freight, it sank in fewer than five minutes. Most of the cargo washed ashore and was recovered. The boat was raised, remodeled, and sailed under the name *Dora*.

Dozens of Flathead steamboats were built. Some were designed as tugs, others as barges. These various ships carried traincars full of wheat, stacks of lumber and all types of commodities.

Stoner's Landing, now Lakeside, was a berth for both the Montana *(top) and the* New Klondike *(bottom).*
COURTESY ARCHIVES, UNIVERSITY OF MONTANA LIBRARY

One of the last ships to be built was the one constructed by Jack Kehoe's father. James Kehoe built the *Helena* at the mouth of the Swan River at Bigfork. Kehoe had come to the Flathead country from Chicago, where he had been a marine engineer on the Great Lakes.

Construction began in July and was completed late in December, at a cost of $10,000. The *Helena* was a lake-type boat, 110 feet long with a 25-foot beam, and equipped with an overhead derrick for loading and unloading freight. The boat rode high out of the water, being 14 feet from keel to deck. Boat timbers were made from local larch, and the hull was covered with iron plate. The propeller was 54 inches in diameter and weighed about 800 pounds. It still can be seen near the Kehoe Agate Shop located near the town of Bigfork.

The *Helena* was primarily a freight-hauling boat without scheduled runs, making trips only as needed. Cargoes frequently included flour, feed, cordwood, hay, potatoes and apples. The boat also moved people and their belongings and occasionally went on excursions, usually from Bigfork to Polson or Big Arm, or up the Flathead River. For James Kehoe, a year's income might have been about $36,000.

On December 15, 1924, the *Helena* ran into the most severe storm ever recorded on Flathead Lake. Carrying flour and apples in 20-below-zero weather in visibility limited to 100 to 150 feet, the *Helena* was unable to get around Angel Point and retreated to Safety Bay at Rollins. Despite extreme low temperatures, not one apple of the cargo was damaged.

The *Helena* represented the end of the steamboat transportation in northwestern Montana. For all practical purposes, this freight-carrying boat was the last to serve the communities on Flathead Lake. It was dismantled in 1932, but the boiler is in use today on a pile-driving barge. With the completion of the highway on the west shore of Flathead Lake in the 1930s, there was no longer any real need for the chugging steamboats on Montana's largest natural lake.

Steamboats on Flathead Lake moved people and commodities, from a brass band and an excursion crowd to a railroad steam engine. COURTESY ARCHIVES, UNIVERSITY OF MONTANA LIBRARY

Jack Kehoe, one of the few who still recall the steamboat era, with remains of his father's boat, the Helena. ROBERT GILDART

Reminiscences of Jack Kehoe

Jack Kehoe probably is most widely known for his agates, but before he established his jewelry store he was an integral part of one aspect of Montana history. For 12 years, from the time he was 14, he spent almost every day traversing Flathead Lake from bank to bank on his father's ship, the steamboat *Helena.*

Today, all that remains of that boat are its hull—sinking deeper into the banks of the Flathead with each spring freshet—capstan, pilot house, several anchors and an assortment of miscellaneous paraphernalia. But Kehoe's memories of that bygone era remain as sharp and clear as crystal.

Jack was born in 1907. For the first seven years of his life he lived near the mouth of the Swan River at Bigfork, where logging was fast becoming an essential part of the valley's economy. But logging along the Swan River was causing heavy siltation at its mouth. Steering a boat through the silt became difficult, so his father bought a new place along the banks of the Flathead River near the hamlet of Holt.

Holt was one of the first settlements in the Flathead Valley. It had a store, a saloon, a post office and a blacksmith shop. As the river was narrow at this point, a ferry carried most of the wagon traffic across the river.

Holt was also a regular stop for steamboats bound from Demersville to Polson, where boats replenished wood supplies for the engines' furnaces.

"Logging was big in those days," recalls Kehoe, "and those were exciting times for a young boy. Huge logs were floated downstream all the way from the Stillwater, clear down from Dickey Lake. For about 20 years, from about 1902 to 1926 or 1927, each spring they'd float those logs by our house."

Logs, according to Kehoe's recollections, were diverted from the bank by a fin boom; other pilings positioned toward the middle of the stream kept about half of the stream channel clear for barge navigation.

Kehoe's memories give a perspective on recent changes in Flathead country. "Each spring," reminisces Kehoe, "driftwood created one of the most beautiful spectacles in the world. But when Kerr Dam was built, the water of the lake raised. That ruined it all."

Kehoe's best memories begin with his father's steamboat, the *Helena.* As an employee on his dad's boat during the spring, summer and fall, Jack did everything. He handled freight, cut driftwood and served as skipper.

One of Kehoe's most memorable experiences began on the 15th of December during the big blizzard of 1924. "We got caught off Mill's Work Dock over across by old Indian Point," recalls Kehoe. "We were running late and Dad didn't like that. Once the river froze, we knew we couldn't get back. At the time, we were carrying a carload of flour and a barrel of apples.

"That night after dark we went towards shore. The wind was whipping out of the south and we were afraid the storm would turn. At seven the next morning, it did just that. It turned hard and started blowing out of the north.

"We got to Angel's Point and the storm increased in fury. A 60-mile-an-hour wind blew and I couldn't get the boat headed north. The boat didn't have power enough, so Dad said, 'We'll have to pull into Safety Bay at Rollins.'

"No wind could hit you there and it was warmer. Everywhere else the temperature was 35 below, but down there it was only about 20 below. Snow piled up on the deck, but it was fluff snow.

"A day later the storm abated and the boat was able to head back toward Holt, pushing through the mush ice. The barrel of apples had been saved by lighting a small fire and placing the cargo next to the heat.

"Back in the valley the blizzard killed several people. People caught out in the storm were unable to get back. All the needles of the yellow pine turned, and everyone was afraid it was going to kill off the timber. But the Indians said no. Said they'd had some experiences that matched the fury of that one."

EARLY TOWNS

Kalispell was preceded by several early towns in the same vicinity. Ashley, a mile west of the present business section of Kalispell, has been called the first real town in the Flathead. It was, in fact, the earliest settlement here worthy of the name "town," the first platted into lots and regular streets. Its post office was established in 1884.

Another town that was short-lived was Demersville, founded in 1887. But during the steamboat era, there were grand hopes for its growth and development. Wrote one early-day newspaper about the then-burgeoning town:

"Situated as it is, at the head of navigation on a level plateau in the heart of the renowned Flathead region, with the grand old Flathead River rolling past its doors, while the silent Stillwater has its confluence but a mile away, is one of the the most beautifully located, attractive and healthfully zoned cities of the great northwest. The lands in the valley embrace a great variety of soils, and have demonstrated their ability to produce in abundance and of superior quality. The scenery in every direction, embracing mountains, woods and water is charming and indescribably grand. With such natural advantages and wonderful surroundings, Demersville is today the embryo of a mighty mart of trade and commerce..."

Such were the fond hopes for one of the valley's first towns, along the Flathead River north of current-day Somers. The town was to become the head of navigation for the steamboat industry that had just begun to flourish on Flathead Lake.

The man responsible for the optimism was T.J. Demers, who had moved here from his native Canada in 1887, intent on carving out a new life.

According to records, Demersville had its questionable frontier characters, such as John E. Clifford. On the night of his election as mayor, he celebrated by buying every last bit of champagne in town at $64 a case and serving every man, woman and child who could stand up all the sparkling bubbles they could put down. Clifford must have further endeared himself to

Demersville lasted only a few years, but during the time when steamboats plowed the lake and ventured upstream to Demersville, the town was the largest in the valley. It died with the coming of the railroad, when residents picked up houses, barns and businesses and moved a few miles to the new site of Kalispell. Inset: T.J. Demers. COURTESY ARCHIVES, UNIVERSITY OF MONTANA LIBRARY

the town's residents when he threw silver dollars and bills into the crowd.

No less a man was the judge of Demersville. Charles M. Sheppard, one of the less renowned graduates of West Point, retired shortly after the Civil War, a physical and psychological wreck. He drifted west, landing in Demersville to become the town's first schoolteacher. Not infrequently the teacher would dismiss the children early and head for the nearest bar!

Sheppard eventually was elected to serve as sheriff and judge. The position enabled him to dispense with certain formalities often associated with the system of jurisprudence.

Sheppard once served justice on a dead man. The recently deceased had that very day disembarked from a boat and had headed for the nearest saloon. Shortly after dark, the new-

comer was shot. The body was taken to Langerman's Saloon and the judge summoned. Upon arrival, Sheppard searched the deceased and discovered a six-shooter and a $20 gold piece.

For carrying a concealed weapon, the slain stranger was fined the $20, which the judge pocketed.

RIVER TOWNS

Columbia Falls

Columbia Fall's first settlers came to Flathead country about the same time as Kalispell's founder. They included "Uncle Mickey" Berne, who died in 1967 at the age of 98.

Mike Berne and his brother, Billy, arrived in the Flathead Valley in 1890. In a 1963 interview with local newspaper publisher Mel Ruder, "Uncle Mickey" told of the town's founding.

"Mickey" recounted how Frank Langford had worked for the Great Northern Railroad in Helena in a clerical capacity. He came to Flathead country ahead of the Great Northern's tracks and founded the Northern International Improvement Co. The idea was to develop the town that would be the Great Northern division point.

But the company didn't appreciate Langford's foresight—and price—so the division point was located first at Kalispell, and later at Whitefish.

Uncle Mickey told Ruder how, to obtain his townsite, Langford "fetched" an Indian woman, Emma Laframboise. The law provided that an Indian could claim 170 acres of land in these parts, and acquisition of land by Laframboise thus took less time than the homesteading process. The townsite company subsequently bought her out, but the name of Emma Laframboise is on every property abstract in the original part of Columbia Falls to this day.

Having acquired the desired property, the company stipulated February 28, 1891, as the date for completion of the townsite survey. Immediately, Mike Berne purchased one site on which he established a brickyard employing eight men just south and east of the present *Hungry Horse News* building. He obtained clay from the riverbank and made the brick for the R.W. Main building (now the Canyon Hotel), the old St. Richard's Church, and the Columbus School, which was erected in 1892 and torn down before World War II.

In its earliest years Columbia Falls had 21 saloons. The most imposing structure was the Gaylord Hotel, built by the townsite company. It burned in 1929.

The town's first post office was established January 19, 1891, with the name Monaco. On July 1, 1891, the name was changed to "Columbia," as fitting for a new community near the headwaters of the Columbia River. Since the name Columbus, near Billings, already was taken the request for Columbia was denied, so Falls was added. The town promoters were well aware of the prestige of having "falls" in the name as in Great Falls and Spokane Falls. But

Columbia Falls as viewed from the east. JAN WASSINK

Columbia Falls has been hard-pressed to find a falls. The nearest one is a still unnamed small waterfall in the spring on nearby Columbia Mountain.

One of the first newspaper owners in the area was John W. Pace. In a January 7, 1892, issue of the *Columbian*, he stated his views regarding the area's prospects: "It is a pleasant and easy matter to sum up the elements of prosperity in the Flathead region, which are, in fact the resources of Columbia Falls."

Publisher Pace included in his listing of resources the inexhaustible water supply from the Flathead River, the limitless forests consisting of the best timber, a mammoth lumbering industry, the finest agricultural region, immense deposits of the finest coal, and oil fields of known value.

Proclaimed Pace, "Columbia Falls is destined to become an important city—the handwriting is on the wall."

Regardless of Pace's predictions, the town did not prosper for almost half a century. In fact, the economy of the town began to sag shortly after 1900. In two census periods, 1930 and again in 1940, the population was recorded as 637. Still Pace's prediction was to come true.

According to Mel Ruder, no Montana town has had a more spectacular economic comeback than Columbia Falls. Following World War II, came the revived and expanded lumber industry; construction of one of the nation's great concrete dams, 564-foot high Hungry Horse; and the Anaconda's aluminum reduction works. Columbia Falls' population increased to 2,652 in 1970. Estimates now place it at a little over 3,000.

Today's industrial payrolls near the scenic Flathead River are impressive and include those of the Anaconda plant and Plum Creek Lumber Company. Other major employers are the Stoltze Land and Lumber Company, Superior Buildings Company, Louisiana Pacific, Canyon Logging Co., Associated Ureco Construction Co., and the Montana Veterans Home.

Residents of Columbia Falls are immensely proud of their town's growth and achievements. Through the years, it has maintained a first class school system. The district high school has an enrollment topping 800, and it's one of the top Montana Class A schools in athletics and scholastic achievements. One past resident, J. Hugo Aronson, a World War I veteran, became Montana's governor from 1953 to 1961.

Kalispell

Hudson's Bay Company trader Joseph Howse built a post near today's Kalispell in 1810, which lasted only one trading season. Eight decades would pass before a permanent settlement was established.

Charles E. Conrad is recognized as Kalispell's founding father. He and his brother arrived in Montana territory in 1868 via Missouri River steamboat and settled at Fort Benton. Before long, he had a thriving freight business. Steamboats linked Fort Benton with St. Louis and freight wagons linked Benton with communities throughout western and central Montana. The freight business was good enough to make Charles Conrad one of the territory's wealthiest men.

On the advice of Jim Hill, an old friend of Conrad and the main force behind the Great

Charles E. Conrad founded Kalispell and constructed his "Conrad Mansion." PORTRAIT COURTESY ARCHIVES, UNIVERSITY OF MONTANA LIBRARY; COLOR PHOTO BY DIANE ENSIGN

Northern Railway, Conrad moved to the Flathead and, with several businessmen from Minnesota, formed the Kalispell Townsite Company. Conrad kept 72 acres, on which he built a 23-room Norman-style house, an extravagant stable complex and a 43-acre hunting preserve. The Conrad Mansion was donated to the city of Kalispell in 1975. It was restored and attracts numerous visitors each summer.

Jim Hill eventually chose Kalispell as the site of the division line and the founders of the Kalispell Townsite Company realized their dream. The 1891-92 completion of the Great Northern across the valley meant the end of Demersville but spurred a boom for Kalispell.

By then, Kalispell had 23 saloons, a half-dozen gambling institutions, another half-dozen dancing establishments, two Chinese restaurants, two Chinese laundries and four

Kalispell and its centerpiece Flathead County Courthouse. ABOVE: JOHN REDDY; RIGHT: KRISTI DuBOIS

general stores. Rhythmic chanting and drum beating by the Kootenai Indians reverberated through town on many evenings.

Kalispell was incorporated in April 1892 and Benton Hatcher, a local banker, became the first mayor. After a single term of two years, Mr. Hatcher moved to Great Falls. There he really cashed in on his new bank cashier job: he was caught after having rerouted more than $140,000 of customers' money into his own pocket.

By 1896, 2nd Avenue West, between 2nd and 3rd Streets, was occupied by more than 150 Chinese people. Chinese truck gardens west of town provided fresh vegetables for stores and restaurants, including four restaurants now serving Chinese food.

A campaign mounted by the Kalispell Bachelor's Club in 1906 to entice single women to the male-filled Flathead attracted the attention of the *New York Journal* and the *Chicago-American*. The club had invited Lotta Varchereau, a Boston pin-up girl, to bring some of her friends to the Flathead Valley. Even the opportunity to participate in a fishing trip to Lake McDonald, a climbing expedition on one of Glacier's snow-capped peaks, a tour of the Flathead Indian Reservation and all the help she needed to "secure a chance for a homestead" did not succeed in convincing her to make the journey.

In 1911, unsympathetic moralists made their first attempt at closing down the 26 of so "ladies of the evening" who made their livings on 1st Avenue West. Although the first attempt failed, another attempt a few years later succeeded. Not content to stop there, the council also banned Sunday shows, movies, pool halls, outdoor privies and vagrancy. The council even outlawed dandelions, creating a fine of $50 for anyone found with a plant growing in his yard.

The base industries of agriculture, forest products and tourism remain the mainstay of the economy of the Flathead Valley. Sweet cherries, Christmas trees, grain, alfalfa, mint, seed potatoes, honey, dairy products and cattle are the main crops produced by area farmers and ranchers. Campers, concrete, fiberglass products, semi-conductor equipment, log homes and plastic molding are a few of the products manufactured by area firms. Approximately 27,000 people live in or near Kalispell, making it the largest city in Flathead country.

Whitefish

Well into the late 1800s, the north end of Flathead country remained wilderness. The forest was dense and the lakes deep and blue. One by one, choice locations were discovered and homesteaded. A man named John Morton was one of the first to homestead near Whitefish Lake. It was 1883 when he proved up his homestead and began to carve a living out of the wilderness. He persuaded his son Neal to come from Michigan to join him. Together, they established a profitable ranching and logging business. Others, like the Baker brothers, relatives of the Mortons, and the Hutchinson brothers, joined them and by the early 1880s, there were several dozen settlers in and around Whitefish Lake.

Soon, other entrepreneurs, like Jack and Ward Skyles, were attracted to the area. They established the first grocery store. In it, customers could find long red flannels, a pickle barrel, penny candy, canned milk and all the other articles considered necessities of life at that time.

For several years the main business was logging and thousands of logs were dropped into the water and floated down the river to the mill at Somers. Concerned with making a living and not overly concerned with appearances, the loggers left thousands of stumps in and around the new town, eventually leading to the nickname "Stump Town."

The railroad arrived in 1902 when a spur line was completed from Columbia Falls. By October 1904, the main line had been rerouted from Kalispell to Whitefish and on to Eureka. The highly desired division point also was located in Whitefish, resulting in a large number of railroad workers following their jobs there.

The Whitefish townsite itself was cleared in 1903. The town was named after the lake, which in turn was named after the abundant whitefish it contained. The town was incorporated on July 13, 1905. A census during that year counted a population of 950.

About 1910, "Weary Willies," "guests" at the Whitefish city jail, were put to work clearing

The former railroad town of Whitefish now is known for its quaint beauty and for providing access to recreation—from boating on Whitefish Lake to skiing at Big Mountain. DIANE ENSIGN PHOTOS

the town of stumps. "If they refuse to work," said the city marshal, "put them in jail on a bread and water diet."

As early as 1935, skiers had schussed down the slopes north of town. The Whitefish Hell-Roaring Ski Club was organized. By 1938, a cabin capable of housing eight skiers had been built, some slopes were being cleared and a caretaker-instructor had been hired. The first Montana High School Ski Tournament was held in 1939 on the Hell-Roaring run. In 1947, Winter Sports, Inc., formed and began operating "The Big Mountain." Since then, a thoroughly modern ski resort has evolved. The annual Whitefish Winter Carnival made its first appearance in 1960.

Today's Whitefish is heavily dependent on the tourist trade. With proximity to Whitefish Lake, Big Mountain and Glacier National Park, Whitefish is gaining international recognition as a premier vacation spot.

LAKE TOWNS

Polson

Lake towns as well as individual dwellings have also established themselves along the shoreline of the Flathead Lake. Polson, now the seat of Lake County, was the site of the first settlement on the banks of the lake. In 1840, one of Father DeSmet's parties came to northwest Montana. A member of the party, a French-Canadian named Abraham Finley, liked the country and began operating a ferry across the lower Flathead River at the site of present-day Polson.

In 1869, Baptiste Aeneas bought the ferry from Finley and built a log cabin. That cabin was Polson's first residence.

In 1880, Harry Lambert settled nearby and began operating a general store that attracted many people to the growing settlement. As a re-

sult of his enterprise, the settlement became known as Lambert's Landing.

In 1884, a man named David Polson, a venturesome fellow from Connecticut, arrived in the area. A talented violinist, he attracted other musicians. Within a short time he was the leader of an orchestra which furnished much of the music for the small community dances in the lower Flathead Valley. When he wasn't off playing his violin he raised horses and cattle, like the other ranchers in the area. The town soon grew enough to warrant a name, and the townfolk selected David Polson and Baptiste Aeneas to choose it. The men settled on Polson. Although David Polson died four years later, the town lived on.

On May 12, 1910, the town of Polson was incorporated with C. M. Mansur, the owner of a hardware store, acting as mayor. With a popu-

Left: The growing community of Polson overlooks shallow Polson Bay on Flathead Lake. RICK GRAETZ
Top: Many Polson businesses have taken a nautical theme to emphasize the city's ties to the lake. ROBERT GILDART
Above: Land-based recreation at the Polson golf course. LAWRENCE B. DODGE

lation numbering 600, the need for a better river crossing became apparent and the Polson bridge was built. Today the town of Polson is a growing ranch and tourist community of 3,000 city residents with another 12,000 living nearby. The city bills itself as the "Port City on Fabulous Flathead Lake" and boasts of fishing, skiing, sailing, boat touring, whitewater rafting, power boat regattas, rodeos, Indian pow wows, a golf course, many fine campgrounds, an airport and room to breathe and grow.

Settlement progressed north along the west shore of the lake. The west shore wagon trail provided the first means of transportation into the upper Flathead area. R.C. Robbin, in his book *Flathead Lake, From Glaciers to Cherries*, relates the story of Eugene McCarthy, who was only 12 years old when his family followed the trail along the west shore. In McCarthy's words, "It was a road in name only. No grading had been done, no rocks removed from it, and the stumps were so high that the wagon axles would barely pass over them.

"The wagon train mired in mud, and three teams had to be hitched together to pull each wagon out. Eugene's father walked ahead to scout the road. South of present-day Lakeside the caravan came to a large, steep hill. To lighten the load, parts of the goods in each wagon had to be unloaded and the horse teams were doubled to carry the several loads over the steep hill. The hill crossing took four days.

"The McCarthys became involved in the business of freighting supplies from Ravalli to the upper Flathead Valley. Whenever the road was talked about, old Mr. McCarthy referred to the big hill as 'Angel Hill' because it was 'so high that the angels roosted on it.' The name adhered, and it is known by that name today."

Elmo, Big Arm, Dayton and Rollins

Between Angel Hill and Polson, lie Elmo and Big Arm, small communities on the southwestern shore of Flathead Lake. Both towns were regular steamboat stops from about 1909 to 1924 and established their first post offices in 1911.

Winter at Polson provides a stark contrast to the hustle and bustle of summer. ROBERT GILDART

A cross-country skier takes advantage of the frozen lake surface to gain access to Wildhorse Island. ROBERT GILDART

41

Top: An undated photo from Big Arm's horse and buggy days. COURTESY ARCHIVES, UNIVERSITY OF MONTANA LIBRARY
Above: No longer disturbed by logging operations and steamboats, Dayton has settled into a slower pace of sailboats and swimming. JAN WASSINK

Elmo was apparently named after a Kootenai Indian called Elmo. Today, the town sports a recreation development site and housing developments that provide homes for many Kootenai Indians.

Big Arm is characterized by its resorts, which allow access to Big Arm Bay. North of Big Arm lies Dayton, a farming community wrapped around its own little bay. Its post office opened in 1893, making it one of the older settlements on the west shore. The old Dayton trestle which still protrudes several hundred feet into the lake from behind the deserted Dayton bank building reminds old timers of the steamboats which visited Dayton on a regular basis until 1924.

Well into the 1930s, railroad cars owned by the Somers Lumber Company could be seen bringing in logs from the surrounding area. The cars were pushed out onto the trestle and the logs tipped off to rattle down into the water. Tugboats herded the logs to the mill at Somers. To-

day the trestle is home for a number of brightly colored sailing yachts.

Rollins, named after Thenault Rollins in 1904, is an intriguing community. The Rollins Landing was busy from about 1895 through the 1930s. In addition, the Dewey Lumber Company of Polson kept a big dock at Rollins for its timber activities. While travelers through Rollins see only Martin's Corner Store and post office, an assortment of recent but frontier-style buildings, and Uhde's Grocery as they stand watch over a bend in Highway 93, the residents of Rollins are mostly out of sight, nestled in little pockets around Sessions Point, Crescent Bay and Dewey's Bay.

Farther north, the landscape changes with rock outcroppings and timber becoming more prominent, but still displaying open meadows and bluffs.

Lakeside

The next town north on the west shore of the lake is Lakeside. It has suffered from something of an identity crisis through the years. John Stoner opened the first post office there in 1901 and named it "Chautauqua," after a popular cultural and religious movement founded at Lake Chautauqua, N.Y., in 1874.

Chautauqua became a kind of generic name for similar efforts to promote education and enlightened understanding at a time when schooling was not always available to everyone who wanted it. In 1896, a group of Epworth Methodist Church congregationalists sought to create a facsimile Chautauqua site on the shores of Flathead Lake. The Rev. W.W. Van Orsdel, affectionately known as "Brother Van," helped acquire some 240 acres of prime lakeshore property at the present town of Lakeside.

The first and only major camp assembly took place in September 1897. The effort soon ran into financial woes. A number of remedies, including the sale of part of the original tract, were tried to keep the project above water. Postmaster Stoner bought the 25 acres, and set up a boarding house that offered popular meals to folks coming out from Kalispell. Continued efforts to launch Chautauqua also failed. By 1900 the dream had faded and the lands had been disposed of.

Somers

At the extreme northwest tip of the lake is the town of Somers, once the valley's second largest community. It was founded in 1901 as a mill town for the John O'Brien Lumber Company and named for George Somers, an official with the Great Northern Railroad for which the town provided ties and timbers.

Somers was the major port on the northern end of the Flathead Lake. It served as headquarters for some of the valley's most ambitious logging operations and as a terminal for passengers and freight making connections between the Great Northern to the north and the Northern Pacific railroads to the south.

Somers became the Somers Lumber Company town and existed as such until 1948 when the vast mill closed. The last remnant of that huge operation, the Glacier Park Company's Tie Treatment Plant, which was being maintained by the Burlington Northern, closed in 1986.

Only a forest of weathered pilings hints at the bustle of shipping, logging and commerce activity that once was Somers. A picturesque yacht basin has replaced it. Many of the sailboats that now engage in racing events on the lake during the year are docked here.

Finley Point, Bear Dance and Woods Bay

Because the terrain along the east shore of the lake was more rugged than that along the west shore, settlement occurred more slowly. With the exception of Bigfork, located at the extreme northeastern end of the lake, there are no major towns on the east shore. The settlements there include Finley Point, Woods Bay and Bear Dance.

Finley Point was one of the sites chosen for the trial planting of cherry trees along the lake. In the spring of 1930, eight men planted several hundred Lambert cherry trees and Black Tartarian pollenizers at several sites near Polson, along the south shore of Flathead

Lake and around Finley Point and Skidoo Bay. These men eventually formed the Flathead Sweet Cherry Association, which later built a packing plant in Polson.

Henry Chapman, a displaced Iowa farmer in poor health, settled in the Bear Dance area in 1893 and founded the Bear Dance Ranch. He soon had enough land cleared for his cabin and an apple orchard. The fallen trees were cut into cordwood and sold to the owners of the *Klondike*, an old wood-burning sternwheeler. When the orchard matured and was producing fruit, the apples were transported to Yellow Bay, loaded on steamboats, and ferried to Somers or Polson whence they rode the rails to eastern markets.

J.C. Wood and his family, in 1891, became the first settlers along Woods Bay. Wood planted the area's first bing and Royal Anne cherry

Top: An early steam-powered lumber mill along the shores of Flathead Lake. COURTESY ARCHIVES, UNIVERSITY OF MONTANA LIBRARY *Above: Lakeside, scene of the failed Chautauqua experiment.* JAN WASSINK

43

trees. He also pioneered the idea of shipping cherries to distant eastern markets. His first shipments, sent all the way to New York, came through in fine shape, establishing a new market for the burgeoning cherry industry.

Bigfork

Just north of Woods Bay is Bigfork. Bigfork Village, as Chamber of Commerce personnel would like to have the town called, has evolved into what is essentially a seasonal resort that booms in the summer and fades in the winter.

Bigfork is located at the north end of Flathead Lake and at the mouth of the Swan River. The center of the town consists of a main street lined with several art galleries, bars, an old and historic hotel that serves some of the finest food in the valley on a year 'round basis, a summer playhouse that has become renowned throughout the Northwest, a number of small cottages and houses, a store that offers high-quality jams and preserves, a filling station, a school, and an inordinate number of real estate firms anxious to convince everyone that those who reside in Bigfork dwell in an area that may very well be one step away from heaven. That may not be far from the truth, but there is a finite number of people the area can hold. Beyond this point the quality of living will erode for even the most tolerant of individuals.

For the longer-term residents, the quality of living may already have begun to deteriorate. Jack and Art Whitney can remember when Indians camped along the Swan River. And one elegant matriarch must surely remember the old country store she had to sell when the new Lake Hills Shopping Center forced her out of business. Since the sale of the Bigfork Merc, the building has seen a number of new occupants. But few have occupied the building for more than a year's running. Like much else that's new in Bigfork, the large shopping center that put the quaint country store out of business is owned by those with more grandiose visions.

In addition to the mall, there is more that has generated controversy in Bigfork. As with

Wheat is one of the major agricultural products of Flathead country. ALAN CAREY

Resplendent in summer, Gatiss Gardens near Creston have earned the admiration of many viewers through the years. ALAN CAREY

Facing page: January at Bigfork "Village." ROBERT GILDART

45

The Bigfork Summer Playhouse provides "big city" theater in a small town. TOM DIETRICH

As summer descends and June progresses, early evening sees costumed performers strolling the village's streets before they gather for performances in another building along Electric Avenue, the Bigfork Summer Playhouse. "Annie Get Your Gun," "Fiddler on the Roof," and "South Pacific" are some of the plays that have been produced through the years. At the conclusion of each musical, actors invariably receive rounds of applause that raise the roof. Actors for these plays come primarily from university Thespian Clubs and acting guilds located throughout the western portion of the United States.

The most conspicuous new series of structures in Bigfork are the condominiums found in the Bigfork Bay—the Marina Cay. These elegant buildings, locally owned, feature a lounge, dining room, swimming pool and time-share condominiums that offer views of the lake, harbor or mountains.

One of the oldest structures in the area is the Bigfork Lodge, owned by Mr. and Mrs. Doug Averill. In summer the rustic log cabin style lodge becomes a jumping-off point for horseback riding, lake fishing, boating and swimming.

Although Bigfork has experienced rapid growth in the past few years, the town remains unincorporated, and there are but a few who would like to see it change. For one thing, the entire area's population of 7,000 *summer* inhabitants drops to a mere 1,500 during the winter. For those that remain, incorporation would mean more taxes, and year-around residents already believe they pay plenty for services received.

Despite the town's growing pains, there exists a genuine aura of hospitality that is special to the Bigfork area. Perhaps it is the result of the area's beautiful surroundings and the somewhat somnolent pace of life.

Shoreline Development

The entire lake shore had been subdivided prior to 1974, when protective Montana state subdivision laws came into effect. Consequent-

all towns experiencing growing pains, school issues have resulted in heated debates. Eagle Bend, with its golf course, housing for retired or seasonal residents, and its proposed harbor, is another issue that created a furor. Nevertheless, the project accomplished much that even some of the old guard wished for: it brought more people into the area without causing too much deterioration to the environment.

Perhaps the most aesthetically pleasing form of industry in the Bigfork area is the Christmas tree growth that lines Highway 35 just north of the village proper. Christmas trees, Scotch pines here, require good sunlight but can tolerate marginal soils. The industry also produces summer employment for high school students. According to teacher/grower Mike Dockstader, it is one of the best forms of farming for the locale, spreading little dust or pollen and producing a high yield on poor soil. Still, what Bigfork seems to do best is to attract tourism.

Bigfork's tourist season begins toward the end of May when the Swan River begins to crest. From all over the area come kayakers eager to run what is reverentially referred to as the "Mad Mile."

ly, there never was any control as to who did what on the lake shore itself. Today, controlled development occurs only behind the first set of shoreline lots.

The lake itself falls under two political jurisdictions—the south half falls into Lake County, while the north half is in Flathead County. Both Flathead and Lake County have lake and lake shore protection regulations to prevent indiscriminate modification. In both counties, permits are required for all construction, fill, dredging and other change within 20 horizontal feet of the high water line.

All new construction on the shoreline must meet construction standards spelled out in the county regulations. However, the regulations can do nothing about existing construction. Flathead County Planner Tom Jentz stated that "50 to 75 percent of the construction already on the lake would not meet today's standards." The situation on the Lake County half of the lake is similar.

A lakeshore inventory of existing development along the south half of the lake was conducted by the Lake County Planning Office and tabulated as of June 11, 1984. The inventory included all taxable properties fronting on the lake. It did not include tribal lands or land held by churches or other tax-exempt organizations.

The inventory covered 339,659 front feet, or almost 65 miles of shoreline. Along this shoreline there are 1,144 docks or a dock located on the average of every 300 feet. The total number of boathouses is 556 or 1 for every 600 feet of lakeshore. Boathouses average 417 square feet in size (approximately 20' x 20'). Dwellings counted total 1,818 or averaging 1 per 190 feet of shoreline. The question naturally arises as to whether there has already been too much development along the water's edge of that pristine lake which the Indians knew as Salish.

The inventory counted 2,012 pieces of property or individual property ownerships. It stated that their average lake frontage was 170 feet per parcel with an average parcel size of 2.4 acres. Of these 2,012 owners, 34 percent are

West Shore State Park. JAN WASSINK

Lake County residents (not necessarily lake shore residents), 45 percent are Montana residents living outside Lake County, and 21 percent are out-of-state residents. Evidence seems to point out that much of the lake shore development occurring now is being done with money from outside the area, and so is not dependent on the local economy. The pattern in Flathead County could be expected to be about the same.

It appears that through good times and bad, development continues. What will the shoreline look like in the next century?

Development along the lake is taking place at a steady pace. Many residents wonder if it can continue without serious degradation of the lake.
JAN WASSINK

THE DAMS

Hungry Horse Reservoir. ROBERT GILDART

Hungry Horse Dam

According to an often-told local story, the name Hungry Horse tells of the ordeal of two draft horses in the rugged Montana wilderness. "Tex" and "Jerry" pulled logging sleighs in the Flathead River's South Fork area. During the severe winter of 1900 to 1901, they wandered away from their sleigh and struggled for a month in belly-deep snow, unable to find food. Gaunt and weak, they were found, prompting the observation that this was "mighty hungry horse country." Tex and Jerry were revived—and the name stuck.

The name "Hungry Horse" was given to a mountain, lake, and creek in northern Flathead country and later to the town and dam located a short distance downstream.

Deep within that concrete dam, a man sits quietly watching a room full of gauges that monitor the operation of the enormous Hungry Horse Dam. The room has an imposing look, but despite the highly technical appearance, operations within it are relatively simple.

"All of the working of this plant could be operated by a single man," says Rich Clark, the Director of Operations for the Hungry Horse Dam site. "That's progress, now, isn't it? Years ago it took 50 men to perform the same task. Now because of computers and other automated features, the entire structure could be operated by one person, though we employ 20."

As a further demonstration of the plant's sophistication, Clark proceeds to a computer room. He presses several buttons and read-outs tell instantly the precise amount of water flowing past each of the 20 dams in the Columbia River basin and the amount of electrical power being generated by them.

"Information concerning the distant dams comes from a satellite orbiting the earth," says Clark. "We are one of the dams in the Columbia River system, so we must coordinate our output with others. Some mornings our dam is operated at full load to generate maximum electricity. At other times it is operated at zero load which we now call the minimum fish water."

According to Clark, the dam produces enough electricity to meet the needs of five cities the size of Missoula. But, equally as important, it serves as an upstream storage area. Water stored upstream can be controlled to help downstream dams to generate an amount of electricity needed by 25 cities the size of Missoula—or in other words—five times what is produced at Hungry Horse Dam.

Even though Hungry Horse dam serves so many downstream metropolitan areas, it is one that has its power source in the middle of a wilderness. On the west side is Jewel Basin, while from the other points of the compass sprawl the Great Bear and Bob Marshall Wilderness areas. Waters from these areas are stored behind a dam that, at the time of its construction, was the fourth largest in the world.

Every dam constructed is unique to the canyon in which it is located. It is designed around a foundation and a canyon. Hungry Horse is an arch-gravity type of dam, meaning that the upstream portion arches outward. The term gravity indicates that the dam tapers from the top and grows larger toward the bottom. The spillway for the dam is the highest morning-glory structure in the world.

At a height of 564 feet, Hungry Horse Dam is an imposing sight. It is a variable-thickness concrete arch structure with a crest length of 2,115 feet. The dam contains 3,086,200 cubic yards of concrete, and backs up water 30 miles. A 100-mile-long rutted road surrounds the reservoir and takes recreationalists to areas that offer excellent fishing and camping.

Work required to clear and prepare the area for the reservoir was massive, although the simple means that were used may still be appreciated. Along the highway that passes through the town of Hungry Horse there is a monument to this simplicity—an eight-foot-

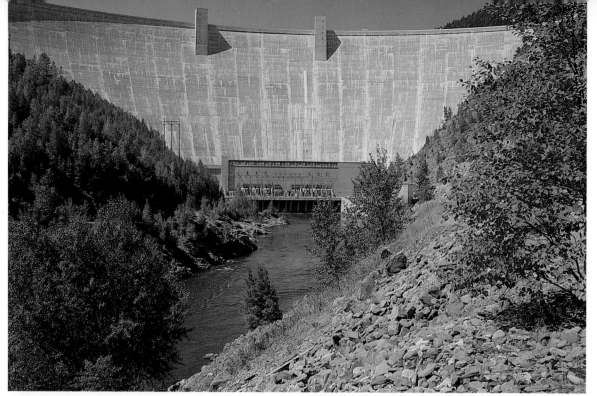

Hungry Horse Dam. RAY OZMON

diameter metal ball made of three-quarter-inch boilerplate steel.

To clear hundreds of trees quickly and efficiently from the dam site, two tractors—attached to each other by a chain—bulldozed their way through the timber on approximately parallel paths several hundred feet apart. Behind them they dragged the heavy ball anchored to the chain. Former dam worker Jim Willow of Hungry Horse recalls that dead snags and some of the trees "snapped off like match sticks when struck by the cable dragging the ball."

While the preparation of the reservoir was in progress, construction on the site was also underway. First, the charging waters of the South Fork of the Flathead River had to be diverted around the site. Then the cement pouring began.

According to Rich Clark, the dam was built out of much the same type of material used by

Romans between 38 and 52 A.D. to construct the Aqua Claudia, which supplied water to Rome. "Romans," said Clark, "used a material called Pozzolan. Hungry Horse Dam incorporated Pozzolan for the first time in America on a large scale."

Clark says that Pozzolan has demonstrated a high resistance to cracking. It also produces less heat when hydrating—chemically combining with water—than the usual Portland Cements. The biggest problem is proximity to siliceous shale. "We were lucky," he says, "that the substance existed nearby in its natural state."

Work on the site progressed at a rate that far exceeded the contractors' greatest hopes. "They're breaking records at Hungry Horse Dam," came a jubilant August 24, 1951, report from the *Whitefish Pilot*. "And they're heading for a new one."

"Only one other dam," said the *Pilot*, "has poured 200,000 yards a month for four consecu-

Inside Hungry Horse Dam, turbines and control board. ROBERT GILDART

tive months. August is the fourth consecutive month." The report went on to say that if more than 200,000 yards of concrete were to be poured again in the following month, Hungry Horse would have equalled any production ever a-chieved on any dam with a single concrete mix-ing plant. The record was broken, but work soon after came to a standstill because of weather.

It was inevitable that some mishap would occur where almost 3,000 men were employed in heavy construction and one tragic event did on July 27, 1951.

According to a report from the *Daily Interlake,* one man, a rivet heater, plunged to his death 113 feet from the top of the dam's powerhouse roof to the bay of turbine No. 4. His fall was unbroken the entire distance down from the roof level to the concrete floor.

Despite setbacks and tragedy, the dam was complete by 1951 and ready to be filled. There remained one last task. When the diversion

tunnel was closed, it caught hundreds of fish in its 378-foot-long passage—cutthroat, Dolly Varden, whitefish, sockeye salmon. Some of the fish were netted and released in the main river and some were taken to the U.S. Fish and Wildlife hatchery near Creston. Then the plug over the diversion tunnel was permanently sealed and water behind the dam was per-mitted to accumulate. For several months, no water flowed in the South Fork below the dam.

In 1952, water began to power two turbines. To-day the site's productivity has been increased through two additional turbines. Water brought in through four penstocks spins the turbines, each penstock passing 80 tons of water a second. Each generator produces 80,000 kilowatts (KW) or 80 megawatts of electricity.

Cheap hydroelectricity power was a magnet for energy-intensive industry like aluminum smelting and the Anaconda Aluminum plant was started nearby in 1955. Initially the dam

was able to supply electricity to the aluminum plant's entire electrical demand. As the plant grew, so did its power needs, and it now consumes about $2\frac{1}{2}$ billion KW hours each year, whereas in normal years the dam generates only about a billion. The additional one and a half billion KW hours come from the big dams downstream. However they would not be able to consistently produce substantial amounts of electricity if it were not for the upstream storage capabilites of Hungry Horse Dam. During the winter months, the dam releases some of the water stored during the summer.

To help insure that the 20 dams in the Columbia River basin work for the best interest of each state, a Northwest Power Pool was cre-ated. Some of the members of the pool are Montana Power, Washington Water Power, Seattle City Power and Light, and numerous federal projects. The Northwest Power Council serves as a regional referee for the pool.

The Northwest Power Bill, passed in 1979, called for the formation of a regional power plan requiring that the source of additional power be determined. No more dams could be built, and so the energy had to come from some other source. The source, believes Rich Clark, has to be the people themselves. "If better more energy-efficient houses are built," says Clark, "that is like building another dam."

Hungry Horse, the Dam Town

Jane, Sue, Mabel, Alice—the girl's name is not important—was inhaling deeply and trying with all of her wind to blow a 50-cent piece out of a shot glass. Behind her, a crowd of well-oiled spectators were placing bets and urging her on. Eventually, the girl succeeded, and a

mighty roar went up that came close to lifting the roof off the Dam Town Bar.

That's about as boisterous as things get now at the town of Hungry Horse. But 30 years ago, this dam town was as wild and wooly as any cow town might have been about the turn of the century. Hungry Horse, to put it in plain words, could be a woeful, wicked town.

Stretching along the highway both north and south were over 30 bars, all of which reaped a good living between the late '40s and mid '50s. According to former dam town worker, Jim Willow, the good living was derived from people who attempted to "run the trap line." The object, according to Willow, was to stop at each bar, have at least one drink and then attempt to survive. Among dam workers, the routine was a tradition.

The rise and fall of such tradition—and that of the town itself—took place over a five-year period, during which Hungry Horse was the epicenter of a mammoth construction scheme. Power was needed in the northwest, along with some means of controlling flood waters that would periodically rise along the Flathead River; they would flood the homes of those who had tempted nature by constructing domiciles in the flood plain. And so the word went out: "Men needed in obscure Montana setting to help build the fourth largest dam in the world." The cry was answered by more than 20,000 applicants.

Although most left after the completion of work on the dam, a few stayed on. Their memories of traditions of the earlier era and their glimpses of life as it was belong in the legends of the Flathead country.

According to residents, the first fire department in Hungry Horse was started during the construction years. Funds for its construction came from gambling and from raffling off firearms. One man won a shotgun, but it had to be taken away from him after he blew a hole in the roof of the Dam Town Bar.

During those days gambling was wide open. A club, Rocco, just up the road from the Dam Town Bar, was built during the construction years, and there were many nights when over $50,000 changed hands.

Jim Willow, a carpenter on the project, has recollections of the rough times of the construction days. "Once," recalls the man, "I stopped my car, thinking the loud noise I heard had been caused by a blowout from my tire. No sir!" emphasizes Willow. "There was no flat. Not far from me I saw a commotion, and there, only a few yards away, was a policeman that had just shot a man through the back. The man had been in the Deerlick Saloon, and he came out chasing another man who had been visiting his wife while he'd been away. All kinds of stuff went on like that. You see, these boomers, as they were called, were heavy-drinking people."

One saloon operator still living in these parts was said to have shot at least three men. He had to, according to Jim Willow, to maintain peace. And the rules permitted. If any unauthorized person took a step behind the bar, he could be shot. That was the unwritten law!

Willow recalls that when he started working on the dam he was making $1.75 an hour. The last year he worked he received $2.25 in union carpenter wages.

"Mabel's," says Willow, "started right about the time of the dam. Girls would come here kind of quietly. You'd see one every now and then getting off a bus right over there near the Dam Town Bar. Sometimes a little boy would be waiting there to pick up her baggage, and he'd carry it on up the hill. Soon the house was in business, and what a thriving business it had." According to Willow, the "house" frequently received about one day's pay from each unattended man with no place else to go.

Willow and other residents say that Mabel ran her house with a close look to law and order. Everyone liked Mabel and residents of the dam town still speak highly of her. If there was a charity, she was the biggest donor. She had a series of houses built behind her house which operated until the mid-60s. Willow believes Mabel will always be remembered, though he emphasizes that he was married and never knew any of the girls personally. But in a small town everyone with eyes knows everything. "Where," asks Jim Willow, "do you think the creeks, mountains and inlets surrounding Hungry Horse Dam got their names from? Where do you think the name Alice Creek came from? Why, she was one of the girls who worked there."

Willow has no regrets about staying in Hungry Horse. "I never made much money, but what a wonderful life I've had. It was a good place to raise a family. I was a scoutmaster for three and a half years."

Willow's four children have all done well for themselves. One is an airline stewardess, another a carpenter in Anchorage. Another of his children, Charlan, serves as an environmentalist in Helena. During the mid-1980s, while plans were being debated regarding the best manner in which to construct the major highway due for completion in 1987, daughter Charlan argued vigorously, but persuasively, for the construction of a road that would incorporate a number of esthetic features. With notable pride, Willow tells how his daugher raised $22,000 to fight the Montana Highway Department and eventually whip it in court

Long-term Hungry Horse resident Jim Willow.
ROBERT GILDART

proceedings through the Ninth Circuit Court of Appeals in California. Still, his daughter never lost sight of her objectives. One was to see that the proposed highway would be narrower by 42 feet. The result is that instead of a highway 120 feet wide, one only 78 feet wide will pass near the town of Hungry Horse. Along its shoulders will be a bike path, bridle path, several small parks and better trails for wildlife. These features will all be an integral part of the construction of the highway designed to parallel the Flathead River.

For her efforts, Charlan was named the Montana Wilderness Association 1986 "Environmentalist of the Year."

Kerr Dam

Few facilities or sites have drawn more attention over the years in the Flathead and Mission valleys than the huge concrete arch dam that blocks the river eight miles south of Polson.

Interest in that powersite dates back to pre-homestead days on the Flathead Reservation, home of the Confederated Salish and Kootenai Tribes. In 1909, President William Howard Taft withdrew all water-power sites on the public domain in Montana from general entry. Permits, revocable at the discretion of the Secretary of the Interior, were available. Because of their nature, such sites weren't appealing to investors.

And so the site sat untouched until 1920, when the federal water power act was adopted. At that time, the Rocky Mountain Power Company, a Montana Power Company subsidiary, applied for a preliminary permit for the site.

But then came more delay—this time due to the economic recession of 1921-1922. The application, pending since June 18, 1920, was taken up for consideration by the Federal Power Commission (FPC) on April 23, 1923. The FPC voted to suspend the application until it received a Department of Interior report on an investigation of the Columbia River watershed.

On May 10, 1926, the government decided to go into the power business on the site and appropriated $395,000 for development of a plant so small that it could develop only five percent of the available water power. An attempt was made by Montana Senator Thomas J. Walsh to withdraw the appropriation in the interests of efficiency, the settlers and the Indians.

Despite the opposition of Walsh and others, the funded proposal was retained. But the appropriate automatically withdrew the land from consideration and from FPC control. Taking advantage of this fortuitous circumstance, the Montana congressional delegation sought to amend the measure so that the government could lease the site to the Indians, who would receive benefits while the facility pro-

vided water and power for all area residents.

By this time it was March 1927. Conferences were held among the Rocky Mountain Power Company, the Flathead Water Users Association and the tribes. The company agreed to develop the large power site, compensate the tribes for their interest and supply power to the Flathead Irrigation Project to replace what the proposed federal plant would have supplied.

A bill providing for all this was drawn up and failed. Finally, in May 1930, the FPC announced that the Montana Power Co. subsidiary would be granted the permit and that the tribes would receive significant rental revenues.

The utility moved fast. In the third week in May, Fox Movietone News camera crews cranked away, filming MPC President Frank Kerr and Indian chiefs at the powersite. The dam was to be named for Kerr.

Polson made plans to celebrate the coming construction boom. By September work was progressing, work that continued despite a series of political setbacks that sometimes temporarily halted construction efforts.

By mid-June 1936, 80 men were at work and the force grew rapidly. In the contract, the utility had agreed to hire a minimum of 20 percent tribal members.

There were, of course, tragic accidents. A coating of ice on the rails made it impossible to brake the work train heading down the hill to the damsite in early February. Warned by the crew, workers jumped from the train as it gained speed. Two men stayed aboard. Their bodies were found in the twisted wreckage at the foot of a trestle.

A month later, eight men died in a slide. In a week another worker was killed and two were injured.

Today, Kerr is considered a dam of distinction. The Kerr Project was the biggest private construction activity in Montana during the 1930s depression. It is a major source of revenue for the Confederated Salish and Kootenai Tribes and is the largest of Montana Power's hydroelectric plants.

The canyon wall overlooking Kerr Dam provides visitors with a pleasant place to hike, an easy descent down a well maintained pathway with steps and resting spots to a rustic vista point, and a challenging climb back up those same steps to the top. The area is also a jumping-off place for the many river rafters who wish to float the wild section known as Buffalo Rapids.

Although the dam is considered important by most Montanans, it became a source of concern for many valley residents during World War II. In 1943, the U.S. Army Corps of Engineers, the Bonneville Power Administration and the War Production Board developed a proposal to increase the height of Kerr Dam. Their goal was to produce more electricity for war-time manufacturing. But one result would have been higher water: lapping at the doors of the merchants in downtown Kalispell and inundating many of the towns along the shores of the lake.

One reaction to the proposal recapped the approval process and eloquently pleaded for the Flathead Valley. It was a letter, quoted in R.C. Robbin's *Flathead Lake, from Glaciers to Cherries*, in July 1943 from then-Congressman Mike Mansfield to President Franklin D. Roosevelt:

"My Dear Mr. President:
"This is the most important letter I have ever written in my life, and I hope it comes to your personal attention because it affects the security and welfare of 25,000 people directly and 50,000 indirectly....

"On June 3 a public meeting was held at Kalispell, Mon., attended by the Bonneville Authority and the Army engineers for the purpose of discussing a proposal to raise Flathead Lake 17 feet by 1945 and 37 feet ultimately. This added water would furnish additional power to Grand Coulee and Bonneville Dams. If this project had gone through as contemplated it would have affected the number of people enumerated above; it would have brought about the removal from their homes of people who had determined to spend the rest of their lives in the Flathead Valley; it would have inun-

Kerr Dam. JAN WASSINK

dated something like 50,000 acres of the best agricultural land in the country; and it would have wiped out some towns completely, others partially; and it would have made a stinking morass of the most beautiful scenic area in the United States. Because of the opposition, and it was bitter, of the people of western Montana, the Federal authorities decided to look elsewhere for added power...but now the Bonneville people and the Army engineers are back in Montana looking over Flathead Lake again.

"I beg you Mr. President, in the name of my people, to do everything in your power to end this uncertainty in their minds.

"Montana had made many contributions to the war through its manpower...but Montana has been treated shabbily since the war started, and many of our people have been forced to leave the state for other parts of the country...

"I beseech you to do everything in your power to stop this iniquitous activity...and to assure the people of western Montana that nothing will be done to alter the status quo there insofar as Flathead Lake is concerned.

"...We look to you for help in this moment of urgency. Please do not fail us."

The future Senator's letter succeeded; upon FDR's intervention, Kerr Dam was withdrawn from consideration.

THE GREAT FLOOD

The Flathead River runs amok on June 9, 1964. MEL RUDER

The disastrous floods of June 1964 in northwestern Montana struck parts of the Hudson Bay, Missouri River and the upper Columbia River basins. The area of severe flooding extended about 200 miles northward along the Continental Divide from Helena to southern Alberta in a band about 70 miles wide. Flooding beyond this area was generally confined to the larger rivers having their sources along the Continental Divide.

The intense rain of about 30 hours duration, falling on the remains of the mountain snowpack, generally produced sharp peaks in stream and river flows, which were the highest recorded at many gauging stations. The destruction of 200-year-old trees at public campgrounds and the uprooting of other old trees, causing channel enlargement, indicate the rare magnitude and extent of the 1964 floods. The estimated flood damage of $55 million in Montana was another type of record.

It would be difficult to design a combination of factors more favorable for heavy rainfall than those of the storm that caused the flood of '64. The flow of moist air from the Gulf was unusual in its direction, and it was broad and undisturbed until its arrival in the area. Then a cold front from the north probably caused a few more hours of heavy rain than otherwise would have occurred.

The record-breaking floods of 1964 and most previous Montana floods occurred in June when seasonal large-scale meteorological conditions may have been similar. Heavy rainstorms along and near the eastern side of the Continental Divide in late May and early June are clearly associated with floods of 1894, 1906, 1908, 1916, 1927, 1938, 1948, and 1953. Mountain snowmelt has generally filled stream channels to near capacity in the same period, and the degree to which floods have been rain-induced is rarely as clear as in 1964. The noteworthy Springbrook storm of 1921 was centered a considerable distance from the mountains, although general rains appeared to have had some effect on mountain runoff as well.

All ingredients necessary for a heavy rain in the affected area were present. Precipitation rates were a half to one inch per hour at Summit. During the period of June 7 to June 8, over eight inches of rain were reported to have fallen in this area.

Rain collected at other Weather Bureau gauges in the valley was also unusually high for the 48-hour period running from 2.31 inches at Creston to 3.94 at West Glacier.

The Flathead River basin upstream from Flathead Lake underwent the most severe flooding in modern times. All main bridges upstream from Columbia Falls were washed out or rendered unusable. Upstream from the Middle Fork, the Flathead River is largely in public land that is sparsely settled. Camping facilities were extensively damaged by scour, silt and debris. Nearly 70 percent of the damage reported in this drainage was to roads and bridges. Peak discharge of the Flathead River at Flathead, British Columbia, near the international boundary was 16,300 cubic feet per second (cfs), or 1,700 cfs greater than the peak recorded during the previous 35 years. Just upstream from the Middle Fork, Flathead River, the 1964 peak flow was double the maximum of the same time period.

Extremely high runoff in the Middle Fork of the Flathead River drainage basin damaged highways and railroads in narrow valleys along the southern edge of Glacier National Park. A natural gas line was broken, and nearly 17 miles of U.S. Highway 2 along both Bear Creek and the river literally disappeared. A steel bridge on U.S. Highway 2 across the Middle Fork of the Flathead River at Essex was washed away. The river flow at Essex peaked at five times the maximum previously recorded.

In the Nyack Flats area, along the Middle Fork of the Flathead River downstream from Essex, 30 residents were evacuated by air. At West Glacier, the main highway bridge to the entrance of Glacier National Park was damaged beyond repair. An old low single-arch concrete bridge was completely submerged, but

Above: The pole line marks the flooded tracks of the Great Northern mainline.
Right: Flood damage to U.S. Highway 2.
MEL RUDER PHOTOS

the arch was not seriously damaged by drift. This bridge was redecked and restored for temporary use.

Flow of the South Fork of the Flathead River was completely regulated at Hungry Horse Dam. Upstream from the dam widespread flooding damaged forest roads, trails, logging operations and resort facilties. All roads in the area were closed because of washed-out bridges or approaches, slides or roadway washouts.

Livestock losses in the Flathead River basin totaled nearly 1,200 animals, mostly cattle, hogs and pets. Three bargeloads of animal carcasses were taken from Flathead Lake and buried in a central disposal pit. Not one horse was in the group.

The June 8, 1964, washout caught a Great Northern train just east of Essex. MEL RUDER

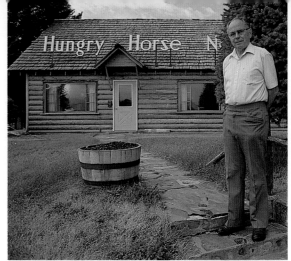

Mel Ruder. ROBERT GILDART

Flood Coverage Wins Pulitzer Prize

Melvin V. Ruder was taking pictures in a barnyard in 1965 when word came that he had just received the Pulitzer Prize. Ruder seemed unaffected and finished his work in the barn. He had just received the first Pulitzer given a Montana journalist. In fact, 20-some years later, no other Montana reporter has duplicated the achievement, and only one other Montana writer, novelist A.B. Guthrie, has ever received a Pulitzer Prize.

Ruder's Pulitzer was for an event that attracted relatively little national coverage. The men, women and children who died during the tragic storm that flowed from the crest of the Rockies were all Indians. Had the deceased been white, there is little doubt that the death knell would have sounded a little louder and the event heralded in banner type from coast to coast. As it was, national coverage was limited, although damage was in the millions and 30 souls perished.

Ruder had been nominated for the coveted award by Montana novelist Dorothy Johnson for his 1964 coverage of the disastrous flood along the Flathead River. The award would be given for Ruder's excellence in reporting, with note to his collecting and sharing news under trying and dangerous conditions during the Flathead flood.

What was it about his *Hungry Horse News* and, specifically, his coverage of that flood that warranted such an award? And equally as significant, what was it about this gruff-sounding man that brought such recognition?

Ruder had founded the *Hungry Horse News* in 1946, a paper that is best defined as being upbeat. Where others covered the sordid activities of the state, Ruder confined his coverage to topics that excluded sex, sin and comics—and garnered Montana Press Association awards for his work.

Ruder is a non-smoker and a man who drinks very sparingly. And his moral principles tolerate no gray area regarding right and wrong. But despite his headstrong ways there are few, if any, who do not respect him.

He studied journalism at North Dakota University, where he was graduated in 1937. In 1942 he was awarded a masters in sociology. Complementing his academic work was practical photography experience gained under Yellowstone National Park photographer, Jack Haynes. Haynes had provided Ruder with an old Speed Graphic to photograph the spectacles of that park. "It was here," says Ruder, "that I acquired a real appreciation for the outdoors." He served in World War II as a gunnery officer and later worked in public relations in New York. But the Yellowstone experience with Haynes fostered Ruder's fondness for the West, and he drove 12,000 miles, looking for a place to locate.

He found himself at Avalanche Campground in Glacier National Park. The next morning, crawling out of his sleeping bag, he overheard two men talking as they were shaving. Their conversation was about a big dam slated to be built on the Flathead's South Fork. "That was the first time," says Ruder, "I'd ever heard the name Hungry Horse." That day, Ruder stopped at the office of the Whitefish *Pilot* and asked about newspaper job opportunities in the area.

Veteran publisher G.M. Moss of the Whitefish *Pilot* commented: "Why don't you start a weekly paper in Columbia Falls? After the dam is completed you can return to teach-

Above: View at the break in U.S. Highway 2.
Left: The Buzz Wyman home in Columbia Falls on June 9, 1964.
MEL RUDER PHOTOS

ing." Columbia Falls through the years had had four newspapers with the last moving away in 1940.

As the years went by the paper grew in stature. Pictures helped make the paper, and photography was one of the reasons Mr. Ruder started the paper in the first place. "The *Hungry Horse*," says Ruder, "was one of the first of the smaller newspapers to depend heavily on pictures." Ruder's philosophy evolved around the "three B's" of pictures.

"It's babies, beauties and beasts," says Ruder. "One or all makes for good news pictures. To that I want to add oldsters."

"Of course scenery has helped also," says Ruder, whose former office is located 17 miles from Glacier National Park, and less than a mile from the Flathead River.

Ruder's paper also grew in stature because of his trenchant editorials. Ruder didn't approve of Food Stamp abuse and said so. Ruder didn't approve of a candidate running for school board and again so stated, and in no uncertain terms. "We found," said Ruder, "that [the candidate] and her husband, in operating their finance company, were making loans to people who didn't exist. I wrote a blasting editorial, and kept the evidence under the mattress at home.

"It's not the function," continued Ruder, "to be the town's nice guy. An editor should state his position clearly, and then stand up and be counted."

Ruder has never considered himself to be the easiest person to contend with. It is a trait which he occasionally alluded to in his columns—and sometimes to members of his staff.

Ruder never expected more of his employees than he did of himself. The only problem, however, was that Ruder seemed to be endowed with an overabundance of energy. On more than one occasion the lights burned 'round the clock. During the 1,700 weeks Ruder owned his *Hungry Horse News*, the paper always came out, though sometimes late: once because of sickness and once because of a mechanical failure. During the 1964 flood, he never slept in a bed, he catnapped at his desk. His wife Ruth brought food to him at the office, which he'd occasionally bypass because of another call about the flood.

Ruder kept going with camera, notebook and telephone. He called the radio station, the AP wire, daily newspapers and, on Thursday evening, came out with his own paper. He increased his normal press run, but even though the tragic events had already been covered by dailies, his flood edition sold out in two hours.

Indefatigable, Ruder continued to write flood stories during the flood week, and printed another edition Friday and yet another Saturday for a total press run of 12,550 copies.

Ruder's paper was considered a prestigious one not only in his hometown community of less than 3,000, but in surrounding areas as well, a test that evaluates the real appeal of a paper. It was circulated in every state, and readers included U.S. Ambassador to Japan, Mike Mansfield. "Once," said Ruder, a world traveler, "I took a photograph of a calendar in a small grass hut in Mexico. It was Glacier's St. Mary Lake."

Mel Ruder owned and operated his *Hungry Horse News* until 1978, when he sold the paper to Brian Kennedy, a young man Ruder respects. During the years he owned the paper, it received many awards. But the most prestigious was, of course, his Pulitzer Prize.

From the time Ruder received his award until retirement in 1978, Ruder never rested on his laurels, though he believes his life was never again the same. "It helped," said Ruder, "to make a good life better." He donated his $1,000 Pulitzer award to the Columbia Falls Library. The fund has grown and proceeds have been used in a variety of constructive ways.

Ruder still writes a column for the *Hungry Horse News*, but now avoids writing about controversy. "That's an editor's function." But Ruder is involved in community affairs and says he may initiate his very first law suit. In the next breath, Ruder comments that after all these years, "he has found peace."

One suspects the world has not heard the last of Mel Ruder.

Phyllis Robinson looks across flooded Nucleus Avenue to her home. MEL RUDER

59

PART III

A RIVER TO ENJOY

THE SOUTH FORK

Babcock Creek, headwaters of the South Fork. RICK GRAETZ.

Big Decisions

There are reasons not to float the entire portion of the South Fork of the Flathead. For one thing, few people have done it. "Listen here," says companion John Schmid. According to Hank Fisher's book *Floater's Guide to Montana,* where the river passes through Meadow Creek Gorge, "The water rushes through the gorge with such great speed and volume that uprooted trees brought downstream by torrential waters have been caught and left suspended 15 feet above the surface of the water...In other places the canyon is so deep that you feel as though you are in a complete vacuum."

Even more discouraging than these admonitions is the inescapable fact that at least one person has been killed in recent years attempting to negotiate this gorge.

But there is a reason *to* ignore the dangers of Meadow Creek Gorge and to float the South Fork, one that takes precedence over all else but safety. That fork of the Flathead is touted by many as providing some of the best fishing in the state. Biologist Bruce May of the Montana Department of Fish, Wildlife and Parks, says the area may contain the best native westslope cutthroat trout population found in the United States. "It's the largest," says May, "of pure native trout whose genetic viability has not been diminished by other species. The South Fork has fish that fight, and in some of Montana's most beautiful wilderness waters."

Accessing the Source

The South Fork gathers its clear summer waters from the spring snow melt off the lofty mountains that grace the Bob Marshall Wilderness. Its official beginning is where the Danaher River joins with Gordon Creek. The location is remote and, consequently, logistics can be a problem, particularly when one must transport large rafts to the source.

Two avenues of access are available. One leaves the Swan Valley and goes over Gordon Pass. The other requires a long drive past Hungry Horse Dam along a rutted, dusty dirt road that stretches more than 50 miles. The road twists, turns and grinds its way around the immense reservoir behind Hungry Horse Dam.

For our trip into the upper reaches of the South Fork, we elected to begin traveling by the dirt road and to stay overnight at the rustic Wilderness Guest Ranch.

From there we made use of packhorses to help make the 35-mile-long trip deep into the Bob Marshall Wilderness where the South Fork has its headwaters. Our two 110-pound rafts were loaded onto horses—along with our tents, sleeping and cooking gear. By 9:00 one morning late in July, we were off, bound for the source of the South Fork.

Two days later, we arrived at Big Prairie Ranger Station, where we met the area's wilderness guard, Gordon Ash. A man concerned about the preservation of his area, he requested that our large party try to find a spot that had not been heavily used before. We complied and set up camp back from the headwaters of the two streams. Then as the afternoon waned and the surface of the water dimpled with rising fish, we quickly assembled our fly rods and selected our flies. Son David tried a Joe's Hopper, I a Royal Coachman. Within moments we each were playing fish that danced across the surface of the water—this was westslope cutthroat trout fishing at its best.

Although the peak of the fishing season normally occurs about the middle of August, the low runoff moved the peak two weeks earlier, making our timing perfect. Our rewarding catch enticed us to spend several days in the area, enjoying our luck and the beautiful country. We were in a broad valley flanked by Cayune,

The South Fork of the Flathead. RICK GRAETZ

Top: Packing in on the South Fork. Bottom: Montana Fish, Wildlife and Parks employees tagging fish for study. ROBERT GILDART PHOTOS

point of each valley. Drifting silently, we saw elk drinking comfortably, spotted sandpipers hopping from rock to rock and relished the sight of the unique harlequin ducks rising with strong wingbeats from crevasses in the river's banks. Most frequently, we spotted female mergansers with their broods. They were doing much the same thing we were doing—fishing. But they could keep anything they caught. Fish kept by human anglers in the South Fork have to be under 13 inches in length.

Before long we encountered several biologists sampling the waters of the South Fork. They answered some of our questions, including why there was a maximum rather than a minimum limit on the length of fish caught.

One of the biologists was Ray Zubick, whom we encountered while he was in the process of catching fish—with barbless hooks, so they could be tagged. From the tagged fish, Ray hoped to acquire information that would help his department diminish the adverse effects resulting from the construction of Hungry Horse Dam.

According to Zubick, tagging fish provides an indication of the number of cutthroat in today's free-flowing waters of the South Fork. From this information, biologists can provide a reasonable estimate of the number of fish that once occurred in the entire drainage, to include the 32 miles of river and 42 miles of tributaries now covered by the reservoir behind Hungry Horse.

According to Ray, the 13-inch limit imposed on fishermen is to permit more fish to grow to a larger size. Some anglers have complained that fish in the area are not so large as they once were. Our group, however, did not complain. The fish we caught were of all sizes, some reaching as much as 18 full-bodied inches. But we complied with regulations, keeping only the more delicious pan-sized trout.

Each night we camped along the river. And each night we attempted to prepare our catch in a different manner. One night we ate fish and complemented them with a superb side dish of fresh fireweed sprouts. In the wilderness anything tastes good.

Butcher and Flatiron Mountains. But one morning we pulled up the stakes of our tents, loaded them into our eight-man raft, and began drifting lazily back whence we had come.

Over the next four days we floated for a total of 35 miles, sometimes amidst the roar of small rapids, at other times through broad, shallow sections where the river spreads. The river's vagaries often created quiet holes nestling behind huge boulders, translucent pools adjacent to virtually every bend in the river and churning riffles shimmering where the river's gradient increased. Into all of these waters we wanted to cast our flies.

Life on the river was different from that of our inbound trip atop horses. We were in a watery environment passing through the lowest

Left to right above: Superb fishing at Meadow Creek Gorge, where our rafting adventure began.

Below: The famous hard-to-find warning sign—high above the river. ROBERT GILDART PHOTOS

Rafting Meadow Creek Gorge

Near Big Salmon Lake we met Curtis who, we had been told, knew the way to negotiate Meadow Creek Gorge.

"It's certainly possible," said Curtis, "to navigate the Gorge. But I haven't always had the best luck during my several attempts. Once, my boat got stuck in the narrows of the gorge and, unable to jar myself loose, I had to let some of the air out of the raft before I could drift through."

Apparently water had poured in so fast the raft filled almost immediately. Curtis was stuck with no recourse other than to release air from various compartments. The raft began to sink, lessening buoyancy along the sides. The man's weight in the middle took that section down even farther until he was in water virtually up to his waist. But letting out the air had narrowed the raft so it could slide through the narrow rock fissure. Moments later the raft was pushed by the current into shallower water where Curtis tediously bailed water until the raft was light enough to lift and dump the remaining water.

On the fifth day, just above Meadow Creek, we encountered the famous take-out sign erected by the Forest Service. The sign perches high on a rock cliff and could easily be missed if one were not alert. We pulled ashore and met an employee freshening the message with a dark-colored paint:

Dangerous waters ahead. Recommend rafters take out here.

About 100 yards below the take-out sign, we encountered water that appeared to be swift, and so we lined our way down the river. Farther along we encountered more rough water and again lined down the river. But at this point our efforts proved unnecessary. We were being overly cautious.

For about a half-mile we floated on, very peacefully, very placidly, until again we heard the roar of the water. Climbing a rock wall, we scouted the area. No huge boulder protruded above the surface of the water, and the stretch appeared floatable. Beyond that we saw turquoise water that appeared deeper than any we had yet encountered. Could this be the place where the canyon narrows so drastically that one can literally step across the river, the raging South Fork that elsewhere stretches almost 100 yards wide? We descended from our vantage point and floated on.

Another 100 yards and the sides of the canyon walls are deeply fluted. The fluting is the result of the abrasive action of sand and gravel. Holes also appear in the rocks where violent spring runoff has apparently swirled like a tornado scouring out the recesses. The indentations are so large, they look as though bowling balls have been excised. In some areas, the holes are filled in with small pieces of gravel. Long ago the edges of the gravel were rounded by the swirling waters. Above the high-water line of the massive 1964 flood, vegetation now is be-

Rafting the South Fork through Meadow Creek Gorge means moving from open waters into high fluted canyons. ROBERT GILDART PHOTOS

ginning to take hold and we saw cinquefoil and harebells.

As we raised our eyes above the low-lying flora, it appeared that the walls of the canyon extended above us for 300 to 400 feet. Gray-colored stone capped the higher reaches of the canyon, melding with soil and the root tendrils of majestic trees. The area is one of sublime beauty. It is unfortunate that so much discouraging literature has been published describing the river as "not navigable," for on this late

Carefully lining a raft through a narrow part of the South Fork. ROBERT GILDART

summer day such did not appear to be the case. The only skills that seemed required for passage were the ability to line our crafts through fast-moving waters, some basic knowledge of rafting and the patience to occasionally remove everything from the craft and portage it around a potential hazard.

Toward the end of our passage through Meadow Creek Gorge we came to one place where the gorge's canyon was so narrow it was necessary to tip our eight-foot-wide craft on its side and shove it through. This area was a deep one. Water did not rush through the narrows, but rather seemed to spurt through. At this point, water is backed up as much as 200 yards upstream. Then it is released.

The most challenging whitewater is beneath the bridge that crosses the gorge. From a half mile above, floaters can hear the roar of the waters slicing their way beneath the bridge. We comforted ourselves with the thought that perhaps it was only the high walls of the canyon creating a multitude of echoes that caused the water to sound so violent. We would find that assessment to be correct. But, initially, the incessant roar was frightening.

There were only two alternatives to continuing our whitewater float: we could completely abandon the raft and return along the shore upstream on foot until a trail up the steep bank could be located, or we could proceed upstream from the bridge, lug the raft up a steep slope for a distance of several hundred yards, dodging trees in dense stands. As both options were vetoed by all, it was time to begin preparing for what lay ahead. Gear was lashed down, cameras placed in dry boxes, life preservers readjusted and buckled securely and rafts pointed to midstream.

Immediately downstream from the bridge, the canyon takes a nearly 90-degree turn. The water crashes against the side of the wall just below the point where the canyon turns. Rafts helplessly follow the raging current, making it impossible to avoid contact with the sheer sides of the wall. Our experience on the Middle Fork had taught us that there is a better way of colliding than simply sitting back and letting the water determine our fate. Rowing against the current to retard the velocity of the craft did not prevent our raft from colliding with the wall. But, a few quick sweeps with our paddles pulled us away from the danger of the turbulence, although we shipped some water. We drifted on, wet but victorious.

Rafter's-eye view of day's end on the South Fork.
ROBERT GILDART

65

THE MIDDLE FORK

Flying in to Float

There are places that seem to exist only in our fantasies; endless areas too pure, too remote, too wild to exist anywhere else. With me, such ideas often take the shape of clear streams that meander and swirl, then tumble and fall helter-skelter through high-climbing cliffs. Sometimes such a place exists much closer to home than ever imagined.

A stream that more than fills this bill is the Middle Fork of the Flathead River—particularly the stretch located within the Great Bear Wilderness Area. Once the area represented an emotionally charged battleground between those for and those against the idea of giving the area a wilderness status. The wilderness proponents won, and today the river remains pristine, its headwaters as difficult to reach as the river is to navigate. In fact, some say the Middle Fork is the wildest of all Montana rivers. At least that is what died-in-the-wool river rats seem to believe. They contend that this fork of the Flathead is the most tumultuous, most awesome, most thrilling of all Montana's navigable whitewater streams.

History also seems to support this contention. The river has cost many people their lives. It has toppled horses and riders end over end bringing them quick death among fields of water-covered boulders. It has ripped rafts, leaving floaters stranded for days without food or dry clothing.

The headwaters of the Middle Fork can be reached by using either pack animals or light planes. Our party elected to charter small Cessnas and fly into a short grass-covered

The Middle Fork of the Flathead serves as the most sublime corridor through the Great Bear Wilderness Area. RICK GRAETZ

airstrip that predated wilderness status. Before descending, our pilot circled the strip to be sure it was clear of grazing moose. We landed and within moments were loading our gear into wheelbarrows owned by the Forest Service and available from nearby Schafer Ranger Station.

This ranger station is an old one, manned since 1933, according to ranger Charlie Shaw's *Flathead Story*. Dick LaVanway was asking questions and chatting amicably with us as we carted our two rafts and miscellaneous gear to the river. He had been working seasonally at Schafer since 1962 when he started as a packer. Now he was working as a wilderness guard. He pointed out that the moose we had passed only feet away was unafraid and still licking at a nearby salt block.

The First Day

After a short haul from the ranger station, we gathered at a point on the river a few miles below the head of the Middle Fork—at the confluence of Bowl and Strawberry Creeks in the Bob Marshall Wilderness. Here the water was almost too shallow to launch our well loaded rafts. We pushed from the shore, and for a few miles we floated on, occasionally stepping into the cold clear water to free our rafts from boulders that could have toppled into the river during winter. The river appeared tame.

Soon the river gained volume. Schafer, Morrison and Granite creeks all had added water to the Middle Fork. Still, the water wasn't tumultuous; the only thing that had changed was the size of the boulders. They were huge, and we regretted that we couldn't have floated in late June, when the water was higher. This particular year had been an unusually dry and unpredictable one; much of the first day was spent pushing rafts off unavoidable rocks. But the fishing remained good, and several in our group of eight men, women and children were avid fishermen. The fishing was excellent, and with reason.

Floating the Middle Fork.

Shafer Ranger Station provides floaters access to the Middle Fork.
ROBERT GILDART PHOTOS

67

In the wilderness the sudden flourish of the water ouzel still contrasts pleasantly with the quiet prowl of the lynx. TOP: ED WOLFF; BOTTOM: ALAN CAREY

Facing page: Harrison Lake on the Middle Fork.
BRUCE SELYEM

This is wild country and, appropriately, the 46.6-mile-stretch of river upstream from its confluence with Bear Creek had been provided Wild River status by Congress. In other words, it is a river that is "... free of impoundments and generally inaccessible except by trail, with watershed or shorelines essentially primitive and waters unpolluted."

For the westslope cutthroat trout, designation of this riverine area as a wilderness couldn't have come too soon. When it was being considered for inclusion, Montana's Senator Lee Metcalf said, "The westslope cutthroat has been reduced to threatened species status due to destruction of spawning habitat throughout its former range... the survival of this native trout species and other important sport fish in the Flathead River system is dependent on the protection of the upper Middle Fork watershed. The Great Bear Wilderness will accomplish that objective."

To test the effectiveness of conservation methods on this species of trout, Lou Bruno and my son David waded waste-deep into water in the Great Bear and commenced presenting their offerings. On one line there was a grey wolf; on the other, a black gnat. Admittedly neither was an expert with the fly rod, and their flies were not always placed precisely. Regardless, fish along the Middle Fork took misplaced flies on the front cast as well as on an errant *back* cast. Within moments both were fighting angry westslope cutthroat trout that pirouetted along the water's surface, then spiraled through the air, and re-entered the water. Rods bent, two-pound leaders strained. Some fish were netted while others escaped.

Among wild rivers this may be an exceptional one, and we were beginning to find that the comments of Onno Wierenga, a guide based in West Glacier, were not exaggerations. Wierenga, one of the owners of the Glacier Raft Company who also runs excursions in Montana and Idaho, compared this section of the Middle Fork to some of the most exalted in the West. "For overall quality," Wierenga believes, "it compares—and may even surpass—the Snake or the Salmon. In fact, it may be one of the finest rivers in the west."

I understood Wierenga to mean that the river we were now floating must also contain water that would put a crick in a person's back if he didn't sit just right while negotiating turbulence. To date, we'd not encountered anything with real foam—anything that roared and had bounce—although we'd been promised that we would.

While waiting for that bounce, we observed that the Great Bear Wilderness is living up to its name. One sensed that, by gazing around at the surrounding peaks. Trilobite Peak had vanished from view, but looming overhead were Arrowhead and Red Plume mountains. Running down the slopes were verdant forests that flanked avalanche chutes. There! That would be a wonderful place for grizzlies. But it was hot, and most intelligent creatures would either be bedded down or cooling themselves in some clear mountain stream.

The avowed purpose for designating this area as a wilderness is best summarized by excerpting a passage from the book *Great Bear, Wild River*, by Dale Burke, well known Montana journalist and former Harvard Neiman Fellow. "To be called the Great Bear Wilderness, the major thrust of the classification battle is to provide the free-ranging grizzly with needed habitat so it can move unhindered to or from either the Bob Marshall or Glacier Park. It further will preserve the watershed of one of the nation's most spectacular wild rivers and its cold, clear tributaries which are vital spawning grounds for the westslope cutthroat trout and the Dolly Varden."

Although helping the grizzly may have been the major purpose for preserving this wilderness, certainly other animals along the river also have been given an extended lease on life. During our trip we saw deer, elk and a variety of species of waterfowl. One intriguing bird is the water ouzel or dipper. This species protects its young by constructing nests in only the wildest of areas: behind waterfalls, or along the banks of raging rivers. Appropriately, we saw a number of these birds on the Middle Fork perched atop rocks, dipping, as they searched the frothy water at their feet for food.

Naturalists say that once a morsel is sighted, ouzels bravely enter the raging water and probe the river's bottom for something that can be firmly grasped in their beaks. Then, with quick thrusts, they snatch the morsel and return to the surface, flitting onto a rock covered with pulsating water, devour the food and once again begin dipping, dipping, dipping.

Nights come early in some parts to the steep-sided canyons of the Middle Fork. The trick is to find a bend in the river that is aligned, more or less, in an east-west direction, still open to the final rays of the sun. Such a spot is even more desirable if its pools are followed by ripples—ideal for trout. Then one can have fish for dinner, a guaranteed benefit of rafting the upper stretch of the river. That's the way nights in the Great Bear are spent, unless the raft has been poorly packed. Then time is spent wringing out water-logged sleeping bags—hoping they will dry over the fire before the chill from the river creeps up the bank and envelops the camp.

The Second Day

One attraction of floating the upper section of the Middle Fork is that the trip can be a leisurely one. From Schafer Meadow to the take-out point at Bear Creek is only about 30 miles. That leaves time for hiking the network of trails that weave throughout the Great Bear, trails that take one to Flotilla, Bradley and Moose Lakes.

Back in the raft, we drifted on, talking among ourselves, applying a bit of sunscreen, taking life easy—undisturbed, unconcerned. We had yet to see any evidence to support the river's awesome reputation.

Early in the afternoon of the second day, the velocity of the river picked up significantly.

Left top: Gateway Gorge in the Bob Marshall dips into the Great Bear Wilderness. RICK GRAETZ
Left bottom: Mt. Stimpson and the Middle Fork. BRUCE SELYEM
Below: The Forest Service cabin raised to these rocks by flood waters. ROBERT GILDART

We had passed many creeks emptying into the main channel, each adding to the volume of the fast-moving water. Since mid-afternoon we had been hung up on several rocks, son David had been flipped out from the rear of the raft, and we'd been slammed into a wall of shale where the raft was swung vigorously through a 180-degree turn. The additional water and the steep gradient of the river, greater than that of any of the other main tributaries of the Flathead River, kept us perking right along.

About mid-afternoon we passed a steep-faced cliff that jutted upward about 30 feet, where it angled to form a platform. A log cabin was perched there. Lou Bruno, a 1985 officer in the Montana Chapter of the Wilderness Association, told how the cabin was uprooted and washed several miles downstream during the flood of 1964, one of the valley's unparalled natural disasters. The boiling water literally planted the cabin on the cliff's 30-foot-high top, where it has reposed ever since. Satisfied with the new location, which is just a short hike from the river, the Forest Service has since constructed a series of corrals there.

While standing near the cabin we heard the rapid waters roar in the canyon below. Downstream, the spray of the water glistened in the afternoon sun creating rainbows. Still, the overwhelming sense was one of sound, followed by feelings of apprehension of a passage that can create such an unearthly roar.

Returning to the river, we rowed cautiously, peering ahead in search of the ultimate source of the pulsating roar. We found it at a tortuous bend in a narrow canyon, where water punched into the side of a wall and then folded back over on itself. A relatively short stretch downstream we could see relief from the turbulence in the form of a sandy beach. We paddled vigorously for the opening, planning to pull over and line the rafts down from there if necessary.

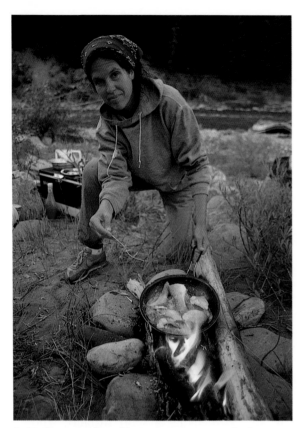

Jackie Stevens of East Glacier prepares an evening's catch along the Middle Fork. ROBERT GILDART

At the last minute we decided to plunge on. Orienting our raft so that its bow was pointed upstream, we paddled against the current, pulling with all of our strength, trying to counter the surging water and avoid having it carry us with it and slam us into the cliff face. Far better to graze the cliff or not even hit it at all.

Raft one maneuvered past the area artfully; raft two was not so successful, grazing the side and shipping a bit of water. Still, all-in-all, a successful passage.

That night we stopped early, anxious to fish a series of promising holes. Later, over a bed of coals, we prepared a dinner of fish for the entire party.

The Third Day

On the next and last day, we rose early. The map showed we would run a series of rapids through an area called Spruce Park. This area, depending on the volume of runoff, sometimes produces waters in the Class V category, which are considered barely navigable. We were barely in the water before that relentless roar once again assaulted our ears, warning us of waters we would want to take more seriously.

Much of the wildness of the river so far had been the result of the steep gradient found along the Middle Fork. It drops an average of 34 feet per mile from its headwaters to Bear Creek. And through the Spruce Park area, there is a four-mile section of the stream which drops an average of 41 feet per mile. This section is the one so anticipated by whitewater enthusiasts.

Spruce Park is an area filled with sink holes, standing waves, whirlpools and hundreds of boulders that challenge both the equipment and skill of rafters. And there is no gradual easing into the frothing waters. Suddenly you are there, and the water is splashing over the bow, whirling you in its eddies, and thrusting you back into the major force of the current. In high water, typical of late spring and early summer, it was apparent that this stretch could easily swamp rafts—or flip small ones end for end. As novices, we were fortunate. This particular year the low, but still turbulent, waters made for smoother though still exciting sailing. By then, we had also acquired adequate skills to do precisely as Onno Wierenga had counselled: maintain rafts parallel to the main flow of the current and hit waves head on.

We followed his advice along the few miles from Spruce Creek Park to our take-out point at Bear Creek near Highway 2. As we unloaded our gear we were convinced that all of our whitewater longings, fantasies and expectations had been fulfilled.

MIKE LOGAN PHOTO

HARLEQUIN DUCKS

Most of the ducks of the Flathead country are associated with the relatively calm water of lakes, ponds, marshes and slow-moving rivers. Not so the harlequin. It prefers the cold swift waters of mountain streams.

Harlequins, the only sea ducks found in Flathead country, spend their winters along the Pacific coast, diving through the breakers for crustaceans and mollusks. With the coming of the spring, they move inland to breed, some of them coming as far east as the Flathead waters. Here they seek out the upper reaches of fast, turbulent, icy-cold mountain streams formed by melting snow and ice. They feed by diving and walking on the bottoms of these streams, searching for the larvae of stone and caddis flies.

The lords and ladies, as the males and females are called, conduct a whirlwind courtship. The lady searches out a suitable stump or cavity in the rocks in which to lay her six or seven buff-colored eggs. With the onset of incubation, the lord abandons the lady and flies back to the coast where he joins other bachelor lords.

THE NORTH FORK

Late evening sun glistened off the gunwales of the canoe as we began our entry into the area called "Fools Hen Rapids." A quick sweep with the paddle and we were around one boulder, but we had shipped much water. Another sweep and more water accumulated. Soon it was necessary to pull to the nearest bank, dump our load of water and begin again. In this way we explored a small portion of the river, exiting at Blankenship Bridge. Nearby was a pullout and our waiting car.

That is much the way in which many people explore the North Fork of the Flathead River—in snatches. A crude logging road parallels the river, although there are areas where one can find solitude, fishing, history, ranger stations and a quaint country store. It all depends on the manner in which you wish to explore the area, and which side of the river you choose.

The North Fork begins in Canada and enters the United States as a boundary for Glacier National Park.

Just south of this area is the old Kishinen Ranger Station. The station is one of the earliest to be constructed in the park and is one that cannot be seen without first finding the correct trail, and then hiking a short distance. Those who find it should attempt to imagine what life may have been like for rangers who patrolled this area in the park's early years. In those times the station was manned on a year-round basis. There was no road and, though some of the rangers found the isolation a delight, others could not cope and asked to be

Quartz Lake in Glacier National Park is a lofty reservoir for water that eventually flows into the North Fork of the Flathead River. BRUCE SELYEM

Polebridge Ranger Station serves as a sentinel for waters that mark the western boundary of Glacier National Park.
Top left: Ranger Susan Kemper at Polebridge. TOM DIETRICH
Above and left: Fishing on the park boundary at the confluence of the North Fork and the Middle Fork of the Flathead, and the same confluence during highwater season. TOM ULRICH PHOTOS

transferred. On a day when dark, low-scudding clouds blanketed the area, one man committed suicide.

Farther downriver—or along the road—one finds brighter memories at the Polebridge Store. The story is of an old country store that has been in operation since 1914. Each year Karen Feather, the store's current owner, hosts an annual North Fork hoedown. In 1984, the event celebrated payment of the mortgage. To help celebrate a debt well paid, a caricature of a bank president was erected on a post and burned. Later in the day, a parade of sorts was devised and North Fork residents marched up the road made muddy by recent snowmelt.

Karen Feather's store is worth more than just a passing glance. The store contains mounts of various species of animals, including the wolf, which is making a comeback in this part of the Flathead River drainage.

Downstream from the Polebridge Merc is the Camas Creek Bridge—a popular spot for the canoeist to enter the river. To the east, Huckleberry Mountain looms. Perched atop this mountain is one of Glacier's last manned lookouts, which motorists or floaters can see from several locations along the road. In 1976 this area was the site of one of Glacier's most mas-

Features of the North Fork include:
Top: Mountains and ponds that attract beaver and a host of other wildlife. GEORGE WUERTHNER
Far left: A post and pole operation near Polebridge.
TOM DIETRICH
Left: A cable crossing just north of the Canadian border. TOM DIETRICH

74

sive fires. Flames leaped across the Camas River road and climbed the steep flanks of the mountain toward the lookout. The fireguard was evacuated and the lookout covered with protective chemicals dropped from a plane. But that was in 1967. Subsequent to the fire, vegetation came flooding back as it often does in burned-over areas. Today, the area is covered with succulent huckleberries that attract one of the densest concentrations of grizzly bears in the United States. Many are the times when researchers, flying over the mountain slopes, have reported seeing more than 20 bears during the course of a brief helicopter flight.

Farther downstream, one comes to Fools Hen Rapids. Here the stream's gradient increases and the water becomes more turbulent. Although the area is challenging and fun to float, canoeists should expect a dunking. The most skilled of boatsmen garb their canoes with splash covers, causing the crafts to resemble large kayaks. Still, they are not immune to the churning water that knocks canoes from side to side and occasionally causes one to capsize. On a hot summer day this is no major concern if canoes have no cargo. Canoes are quickly turned upright and floaters continue, occasionally proceeding to the head of Flathead Lake.

Top: The pole bridge over the North Fork at the town of Polebridge. EMANUEL SCHLABACH
Far right: Karen Feather, proprietor, poses in front of her Polebridge Mercantile. TOM DIETRICH
Right: Bowman Lake on the North Fork. BRUCE SELYEM

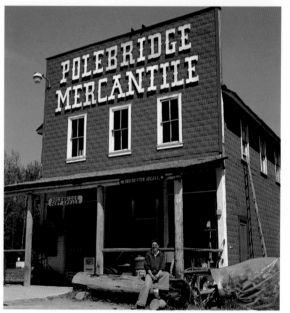

LAKE COUNTRY

Lake country is an area that remains pristine wilderness despite the encroachment of ranches, farms and unchecked subdivisions. It is an area from which one can learn of nature—past and present. It is also an area to enjoy and explore.

Lake Islands

Both old-timers and personnel from the Montana Department of Fish, Wildlife and Game (MDFWP) say that the islands near the mouth of the Flathead River are sinking. Sandbars now lie where islands once jutted from the water. The bars served as a beach-head in a futuristic George Peppard motion picture a few years ago. In the movie, Peppard and survivors of a Hollywood-produced holocaust rise from Flathead Lakes' mysterious depths and come ashore in an amphibious tank.

Another island, near this group and west of Bigfork, is called Doc's Island. The private island is adjacent to the Migratory Waterfowl Refuge. To protect the nesting zones, most of the area is off-limits to the public.

In the Somers area are several small islands. The largest is Rognilie's Island. When the Somers Lumber Company built an extensive maze of harbor pilings to support its buildings, it incorporated the tiny island in the structures. The steamboat *Willis* sank near here in 1941. Off Somers Beach rises Hog Island, a perpetually windy spit of rock marked by what appears to be a flagpole base. Rumor has it that a navigation beacon or similar device operated off this island. Hog Island offers a good spot from which to watch sailboat races.

Along the west shore, south of Somers, the first island encountered is Goose Island, the first of a series of posted, off-limits nesting rocks that are of major importance to Canada geese and other users of the Pacific Flyway.

Goose Island, seen here from West Shore State Park, is posted to avoid disturbing the nesting Canada geese. JAN WASSINK

76

According to local sources, Flathead Lumber Company maintained a dock near the island in the late 1800s. In fact, there were a series of steamboat docks all along the west shore as far south as Table Bay. The Douglas Island and particularly Mary B. Island off Table Bay are of interest to MDFWP personnel as goose nesting grounds.

Off Painted Rocks Point and Dewey Bay are Cedar, Shelter and Rock islands. The state purchased 23.6-acre Cedar Island in 1954, and MDFWP manages it as a wildlife preserve. The other two islands are privately owned.

Various business ventures had structures on these three islands. From the late 1800s to the early 1900s, steamboat docks marked the shoreline from Rollins to Dayton. Other enterprises were represented including Kalispell Mercantile, Dewey Lumber Company, Tripps' Landing and Somers Lumber Company.

Farther south is Cromwell Island, the lake's second largest. Located off Blackbird Point close to Wildhorse, the island is the property of lake historian Thain White.

The third largest lake island is Melita Island. Located off Big Arm Bay, Melita was once a Boy Scout summer camp. The island is now private property. Near Melita is Dream Island, smallest island in the Wildhorse Island group. It is owned by the descendants of copper magnates from Butte. The steamboat *Pocahonttas* sank off Dream Island in 1888.

The most extensive of the islands is the Narrows group: Narrows Island, Big Bull Island and Little Bull Island. This group is located in the narrow channel between shallow Polson Bay and Flathead's deeper main water to the north. Steamboat traffic was heavy through the Narrows around the turn of the century. The steamboat *Somers*, out of Polson, sank off Stone Quarry Point in 1919.

Directly north of Finley Point are the Bird Islands, which are managed by the University of Montana Biological Station. Director Dr. Jack Stanford points out that what may seem like barren piles of rocks are actually offshore gathering places where wildfowl are not bothered

Above: Wildhorse Island, now managed as a state park. Left: Tundra swans rest on the lakeshore on their way north. JAN WASSINK PHOTOS

by humans. Here they have a chance to complete their natural growth patterns.

Wildhorse Island—the Largest

Approximately 10,000 years ago, the seemingly irresistible force of the Flathead Glacier met an immovable object in the form of a large mass of igneous rock. The immovable object prevailed, forcing the glacier to move over and around it. Less resistant land surrounding the object was scoured away.

That immovable object exists today as Wildhorse Island and guards the lake entrance to Big Arm Bay on the west side of Flathead Lake.

According to one account, the origin of the island's name dates back to the early 1700s, long before white men arrived on the scene. The Kootenai Indians were losing horses to Blackfeet raiders who crossed over the mountains that are now in Glacier National Park and came down the Middle Fork drainage. Whenever a band of marauding Blackfeet was spotted, the Kootenai would drive their horses into the grey-blue glacial waters of Flathead Lake and over to the island. After the Blackfeet left the vicinity, the Kootenai attempted to round up the horses and swim them back to the mainland. The 2,156-acre island provided hiding places for half-tamed horses and many horses were overlooked and left behind. Those animals soon reverted to their natural state, thus the name "Wildhorse Island."

Possession of land was 100 percent of the law until 1904 when Congress authorized a survey of reservation lands to establish "legal" ownership by Indians. Originally, all islands in the Flathead Lake were part of the Indian reservation, but as of 1904 each Indian was to be allowed an allotment of land, 80 acres if the land was good, up to 160 acres if the land was less desirable. The most desirable land, particularly lakeshore, was to be divided into two- to five-acre villa sites.

After the Flathead tribal members had made their requests for allotments, non-Indians were offered homesteads by a lottery system. Fewer than 20 percent of the applicants under the lottery system actually appeared to claim their land. In 1910, the remaining unclaimed land on the reservation was opened to homesteading under "squatter's law."

Herman Schnitzmeyer was one of the first of many to try his luck on the island. Within four years, he had given up and moved to Polson to start a photography business. Other island homesteaders included a cattleman named Roy Tonkinson; the Norbert family; dairy farmers, who also made the mail run between the island and Dayton; W.A. Powers; A. Thurber; Jim MacDonald; and a Mr. Graves.

After the homesteaders failed to make a go of it, the federal government again stepped in and put much of the island up for sale in a surplus-land auction in 1915. Col. Almond A. White purchased more than half of the villa sites on the island. He also purchased most of the interior parcels at $15 an acre but had to go as high as $50 an acre for several of the better parcels. White's purchases amounted to $75,000 of the total $130,000 raised by the sale. Buyers were permitted to make a down payment and put the remainder on time payments.

A man of vision, White planned to establish on the island a boys' school, a resort hotel, a game refuge, a power plant and the world's largest observatory. With that in mind, the Minnesota native went to work. Even free excursions from Glacier National Park for prospective buyers failed to elicit the desired sales and most of his property eventually went back on the auction block in lieu of delinquent payments and taxes. His vision of a summer wonderland for tourists was bright; it was just one depression and three wars too soon.

The Reverend Robert Edgington was the next person to try his hand at making a living off the island. He constructed Hiawatha Lodge and, in 1931, began operating a dude ranch on the east side of the island. The clientele, mostly wealthy eastern tourists, were given free run of the island to enjoy the scenery and observe the wildlife. All went well until October 1934, when a violent storm struck. Huge waves rolled over the Edgington dock and threatened to make kindling of the boats tied there by hurling them against each other and the dock. Mr. Edgington and his caretaker fought to save the boats but were both swept into the angry water. The caretaker made it back to land, Mr. Edgington did not.

Soon after, Lewis Penwell of Helena bought the island and tried to continue the dude ranch. He completely renovated the Hiawatha Lodge, added a large dock and launched a 150-horsepower boat so his clients could cruise the lake or water ski if they wished. Without Edgington's eastern connections, the business faltered, and by 1941 Penwell stopped entertaining guests. Instead, he decided to establish a game preserve. In spite of the fact that deer and large numbers of blue grouse were already inhabiting the island, he petitioned the Montana Fish and Game Commission for permission to stock deer, elk, bighorn sheep, pronghorn and game birds. By the end of the year, wild turkeys, pronghorn, deer and game birds had all been planted on the island and seemed to be thriving. Shortly after that, Penwell set about to acquire the whole island, a task he accomplished by 1943 with the exception of one tract—the biological plot owned by the State and designated to be used by the Natural Science Department of the University of Montana.

On September 8, 1943, all of Penwell's island holdings were purchased by Dr. J.C. Burnett for a sum believed to be between $90,000 and $145,000, making it one of the largest real estate transactions in western Montana as of that time. Dr. Burnett immediately went about buying good-quality mares, a purebred Arabian stallion, and a thoroughbred stallion named Riskulus, which had set a track record for the mile and one-eighth as a four-year-old and cost Burnett well over $30,000. Problems from range use would soon occur.

After the state legislature passed a law allowing the university to exchange island land for other land, Burnett traded the university for the remaining tract on the island and became the first man to own the whole island.

Overgrazing by Burnett's horses and the wildlife on the island resulted in depletion of the vegetation. The dry summer of 1955 compounded the problem, and all the animals on the island went into the winter in poor condition. Late October marked the first of many winter storms. The island was besieged for weeks at a time by bitterly cold arctic air masses accompanied by howling winds. A layer of ice an inch thick crusted over the snow, making it harder for grazing animals to reach what little grass was left beneath. Members of the Polson Saddle Club became concerned about the horses on the island. Andy Blades, Bob Lynn and Harold Seifert went to the island to check and found the horses so desperate for food that they were eating sagebrush stems up to one and one-half inches in diameter. The saddle club members obtained permission to begin "Operation Hay Lift." In spite of the airdropped hay, only two horses and a mule survived the winter. After Burnett's death in 1959, they, along with the island, went up for sale.

Considerable public debate was sparked when the University of Montana, hoping to purchase the property for use in wildlife research, competed with the eventual purchaser, a Butte businessman named Bourke MacDonald. Concerned with protecting the wildlife, MacDonald worked closely with the Montana Fish and Game Department. He opened the island to the public for photography but banned dogs,

smoking, campfires and hunting. He soon announced plans to sell 166 lots on the south and west shores. He also planned to develop coves on the east and north shores for public access. Strict covenants were established to preserve the island's natural character. Fortunately, only 49 lots were sold. But, 14 cabins still exist on the island.

After the death of Bourke MacDonald in 1973, his heirs sought a buyer who would ensure long-term preservation of the island as a resource for future generations of Montanans to enjoy. The island had a bald eagle nest, bighorn sheep, the native palouse prairie and a ponderosa pine forest. These resources interested the Nature Conservancy, a nonprofit organization concerned with protecting the habitat of rare and endangered species of plants and wildlife.

The MacDonald family proposed to donate one-half of the island's 1977 fair market value of $3.5 million to the state of Montana. Under certain circumstances, the Department of Fish and Game could match donated land value dollar for dollar with the Federal Land and Water Conservation Fund.

This proposal was presented to Gov. Thomas L. Judge and the 1977 Montana Legislature. The legislature responded by passing H.B. 836, which mandated the island's purchase as a state park, if necessary federal or private funds could be secured, and contained authority to spend up to $2 million of such money for the purchase. Governor Judge signed the bill into law. With that signature an island that was subjected to grandiose get-rich-quick schemes for more than 70 years was placed out of reach of the profit motive. The palouse prairie, bald eagle and bighorn sheep are now protected from the lure of the dollar. Another rare plant, the Columbia River crazyweed, has since been dis-

covered on the island by the Nature Conservancy and was protected by a voluntary agreement with the landowner where it was found.

In March of 1982, the old brown mule died. His companion for over a quarter of a century, a 27-year-old black Arabian stallion, survived but seemed unusually restless. He spent his days walking the island. Each evening, he drank from the bay near the dock.

Concerned about the lonely old stallion and unable to picture Wildhorse Island without horses, the Montana Department of Fish, Wildlife and Parks transplanted three geldings to the island on October 3, 1982. The three new residents, a 17-year-old chestnut, a 13-year-old grey pinto and a 9-year-old bay, were rounded up near Rock Springs, Wyoming, and came to Montana through the Bureau of Land Management's "Adopt a Wild Horse" program.

The old stallion died in 1985 but the remaining horses guarantee that the image of Wildhorse Island will remain intact.

Flathead country offers activities to please everyone.
Top left: A young nature "photographer." JAN WASSINK
Above: The town of St. Ignatius. RAY MILLER
Far left: BMX racing at Kalispell. JAN WASSINK
Left: Windsurfing on Flathead Lake. JAN WASSINK

80

Clockwise from below:
Rafting. ROBERT GILDART
Snagging for salmon on the Middle Fork (no longer permitted). TOM ULRICH
A January scene of the frozen Flathead Lake. KRISTI DuBOIS
Enjoying Flathead Lake. JAN WASSINK
Kayaking the "Mad Mile." JAN WASSINK
Stanton Lake and Great Northern Mountain on the Middle Fork. BRUCE SELYEM

Above: An old barn presents a peaceful scene on a July afternoon by Flathead Lake. JEFF GNASS

Moderated by the almost 200 square miles of open water of Flathead Lake, the climate is ideal for growing cherries. An estimated 65,000 cherry trees ring the lake. ROBERT GILDART

Cherry Country

Fertile glacial soil and moderate winter temperatures resulting largely from the 197 square miles of open water of Flathead Lake make the lake's shore the only area in Montana suitable for commercial cherry culture. About 95 percent of Flathead cherries are grown on the east shore, where the prevailing winds deliver the warming temperatures of the lake. The presence of this large body of water keeps the valley from experiencing the rapid temperature changes prevalent in most of Montana. Although it is said to freeze on a ten-year average, the lake froze in 1979 and again in 1985 and 1986.

Cherry growing began in the early 1920s. Oscar Moen is credited with being one of the first planters. But the industry didn't get into full swing until the spring of 1930 when eight Polson area men pioneered the industry by planting several trees on the hills east of Polson on Finley Point near Skidoo Bay.

In 1935 a Cherry Growers Association was organized to facilitate packing, hauling and marketing. By 1944, there were 60 acres of cherry trees and more than a million pounds of Flathead cherries were on the market. By 1981 the seasonal average was 4 million pounds of delicious cherries. The Flathead Lake Cherry Grower Association Plant produced 6 to 7 million pounds in 1985.

The improved taste and increased harvest are results of research sponsored in part by the various cherry growers associations. Rain, according to researchers, followed by sun when the cherries are ripe, causes them to split. A crop can become almost worthless in a day's time. But researchers have discovered that the application of rosin, fish oil, soap and casein, tannic acid, boron and calcium may seal off or toughen the cherry surface so moisture cannot penetrate.

Today, there are about 600 cherry orchards in Flathead County and about 1,400 in Lake County, averaging about one to one-and-a-half acres in size. The largest is about 15 acres. Assuming 100 trees to the acre there are about 65,000 cherry trees on the Flathead.

Hans Gronke, who operates a cherry orchard near Bigfork, said that after clearing and cultivating the ground and building a substantial deer- and people-proof fence, cherry growers then plant the small trees and continuously cultivate the surrounding soil. He added, "And that's not the end for I have to constantly replant them when they die or become unproductive, after about 10 years. Though on rare occasions, some trees live as long as 30 years."

Growers must work constantly at controlling disease, insects, rodents, weeds, deer and bears; and pruning, fertilizing, irrigating, preventing sun-scald to tree trunks, harvesting, handling, transporting and marketing. At any time, about one tenth of an orchard is being replanted.

Pollination is the task of honey bees. Hives are either purchased or rented by growers with rentals costing about $14 to $15 per hive each season. Since bees work only during warm and sunny days, a cold, wet spring can be disastrous.

Most orchards are on a five- to seven-day spraying program during the season, which is from before blossom to harvest. Fruit flies begin to show up in early June. Spraying is curtailed well before harvest and during the pollination period lest the bees be harmed.

The problems confronting the cherry growers are numerous, many at the moment of harvest. Phil Pruzzo and his wife, Colleen, have been growing cherries for 10 years and are well able to describe late-season problems The couple raises about 50 trees per acre. Each of the Pruzzos's trees produces about eight to 12 boxes of cherries.

"It is all-important," says Phil, "that cherries be picked a little on the pink side so that they will remain firm during transport. Immediate cooling en route to the packing plants is best. Plants are becoming computerized for sorting and grading. We've also got better methods of cooling and maintaining temperature controls while the fruit is being shipped to the consumer."

Because the pollination of cherry orchards such as this one depends upon honey bees, cold wet spring weather that limits bees' activity can mean a poor crop year. JAN WASSINK

Not all of Pruzzo's fruit goes to the consumer. Cherries make delicious wine, though in Pruzzo's case, it is only for family and friends.

Cherries from the Pruzzos' orchard are shipped all over the country. Some of the national food chains buy their cherries, which include four of the different varieties found along the Flathead: Lambert, Royal Anne, Decon, Van. Other varieties include Rainier, Bing, Tarts and Golden Stark.

For Phil and Colleen Pruzzo, 1985 was one of the best years since they began raising cherries in 1975. But just one mile up the road the situation was different. The previous night, it had hailed and the cherries had split.

"Raising cherries is a fickle business," say these two cherry farmers. "You need a dry season, and good pollination, which means the bees have to be working just right.

"I guess ideal conditions prevailed for us."

A bountiful harvest of Flathead cherries. RAY OZMON

Cherry Pickers

Imagine fruit growing so densely in Montana that branches must literally be supported with props to prevent the overloaded limbs from shearing off their trunks. The picture is even more impressive when one realizes that the fruit is cherries—cherries growing so profusely that from a distance that, on sun-filled days, branches seem to shine and glimmer with a reddish glow.

That's the way fruit grows along the shores of Flathead Lake, where the harvest attracts approximately 300 migrant workers during the summer months.

Some of the workers are Mexicans who have crossed the Rio Grande on a moonless night and worked their way north. En route they hope they will not be checked to determine if they have the appropriate "green card" that will enable them to work legally. There are also families who have been following the harvest now for several generations, such as the Kincaid clan, who pick for the Pruzzos. For them it is a family affair and, they say, "We wouldn't dream of doing anything else."

Typically a season for the Kincaids will start in Stockton, California. From there, they will work their way north, progressing to Kennewick, Quency, Desert Air and Wenatchee, Washington, and on to Lakeside, Montana. They then head to Washington for the apples and return to Arizona where they winter, waiting for the next season.

"My children married fruit-picking people," says Jurdene Kincaid. "I've been a fruit picker for at least a couple of decades. But I wouldn't advise the migrant life for anyone. Family members on my husband's side have all died young. Several years ago my husband died. He was only in his 50s."

Fruit pickers are also having trouble keeping up with inflation. And, too, they must contend with illegal aliens who can underbid them. But most orchard owners won't hire aliens unable to prove they are legal residents.

"We're like many other pickers," says Jurdene. "We realize the Mexicans who come north have to eat. But so do we. And then, this is our country. If the workers are here legally, we don't mind working right along with them. But the ones who are here illegally, they're stealing work from citizens of the United States. Some cherry pickers have started a sort of vigilante committee."

With a contemplative look in her eyes, Jurdene continued, "Not everyone is geared for this type of work. Cherry picking is an art. You just can't get someone off the street and say 'go pick cherries.' They'd never be able to do it. It takes a certain breed, someone who doesn't mind living in a camper, a tent or travel trailer for six months out of the year. That's the way we live while on the road."

Jurdene's daughter Sherri and her husband are in their 20s and have the strength and stamina to withstand a life of constant change. They've never known anything else. Ron manages crews and Sherri is said to be one of the fastest pickers in the business. In the course of a single hour, Sherri may pick seven boxes—which means she plucks about 5,000 cherries an hour. The average person picks only about four to five boxes, while the slowest may pick only two or three an hour.

"Good cherry pickers," says Sherri, "take hold of the stem and pull it to them. By so doing they prevent the cherries from losing their stems and 'bleeding.' The leaves are taken and simultaneously discarded."

Picking is hard work and it seems to show up first in the picker's hands. Occasionally, a raw cherry will break in her fingers or palms and stain them purple. Beneath her nails and embedded in the lines of her hands is dye from the leaves and juice from the fruit. Sherri is fortunate that, in her mid-twenties, she is youthful and healthy. Others in her profession have faces furrowed from too much sun.

According to Sherri, one asset of her family's lifestyle is its continual close association. "Our kids are off the streets and with us. If my daughter's children follow suit, we'll always be a very close-knit family."

Left: Many non-residents make annual pilgrimages to the Flathead to pick cherries. MICHAEL S. CRUMMETT
Above: Sherri Kincaid's family has been picking cherries for several decades. Not afraid of hard work, she emphasizes that following the cherry harvest has kept them a close-knit family. ROBERT GILDART

THE MAD MILE

Boulders line the Swan River near Bigfork, prominent ones as well as hidden ones; about the only thing that can be said favorably about their presence is that they are smooth and rounded by the torrents of rushing water.

Much of this action takes place in spring when heavy snow melt from the mountains is at its peak flow. Objects caught in this sweep of water are carried along, perhaps disappearing into one of the maelstroms along the way, or weeks later, drifting into the bay at Bigfork.

But there is a way to venture through this area between the dam on the Swan and Bigfork Bay—an area popularly referred to as the "Mad Mile" by those who have learned to negotiate it. Not just anyone can climb into a kayak and maneuver it safely through this turbulent water. To do so requires skill honed to such a fine edge that all actions come automatically,

The boulder-strewn Mad Mile tests skill, endurance and equipment. ROBERT GILDART PHOTOS

for there are many stretches that test the skill of even the most experienced white-water buffs.

The first White Water "Mad Mile" kayak gathering was organized in 1974 by Cliff Person of Whitefish. Since that time the contest has come a long way. In 1980, the Bigfork Area Chamber of Commerce began a May White Water Festival in response to interest in the activity.

Complementary events were instituted by the Chamber, including a triathlon, criterion bike race, barbecue and helicopter rides. In fact, the event has proven so successful that in recent years Governor Ted Schwinden declared Bigfork the "White Water Capital of Montana."

Waters that attract floaters are commonly categorized according to their degree of difficulty from I to VI with I being considered as ripples and VI being considered so difficult that navigation is virtually impossible. An example of Class VI waters would be those found in the spring on the Meadow Creek Gorge near the Bob Marshall Wilderness. Class IV waters are defined as one with "big numerous waves and very fast current." Careful inspection of the river's course is essential. Waters such as these require advanced to expert levels of particular skills.

The Mad Mile includes waters from Class I through Class IV or V, depending on the heaviness of the spring runoff.

Some specific areas have received honorary designations from participants. Consider, for example, the "Moe Hole," along the Swan, where Tom Moe got caught in 1975, lost his paddle and had his boat broken into a dozen or more pieces. Says expert kayaker Cliff Person, "The 'Moe Hole' is treacherous. You're on the crest of a wave with the sun shining in your face and then, suddenly, you're dropped into a hole and thrashed about."

To add spice to the Bigfork White Water Festival, the course along the Swan River includes two major types of racing. One race is timed over the entire course. The other is a slalom event where the participant must per-

Excitement on the river (facing page) and the Mad Mile's related events, including vintage automobiles and a carnival atmosphere. ROBERT GILDART PHOTOS

form a number of maneuvers. In this contest, kayakers must negotiate through a downstream gate, a reverse gate where the stern of the craft passes through the gate first, and an upstream gate where the participant turns in below the gate and passes upstream through the gate bow first. Says Cliff, "The gates are mixed up into a combination to make the course as difficult as possible."

Until recently no one has been hurt. But in 1986, on the day of the event, a woman kayaker was drowned sometime in the late evening while practicing, navigating the river alone and unwatched.

JEWEL BASIN: GEM OF THE SWAN

My son commented afterwards that the worst part of the journey was probably the drive to the jumping off point at Noisy Basin, which we accomplished in the comfort of our automobile while worrying mostly about ripping the sidewall of a tire on the rocky climb to the parking area. The road was rough, but navigable if taken slowly, and well worth the result.

The hike into Jewel Basin was a breeze. Forty-five minutes after leaving the car we finished the hardest uphill climb, which took us to the trailhead for Black Lake and Picnic Lakes (to the north)—and Birch Lake and Crater Lake (to the southeast), the direction we chose. Within an hour we had shed our backpacks and were fishing in the dappled, sunlit waters of Birch Lake on the southern flank of Mount Aeneas.

Inclusive of the drive from Bigfork, the journey to Birch Lake had taken fewer than three hours while providing us with a panoramic view of Flathead Lake and the lower valleys as well as the Swan and Mission mountains stretching to the south. The walk to Birch Lake from the trailhead was mixed uphill and downhill hiking, but not tiring, and had taken us through flower-filled meadows and glades and along hillsides, offering us views of rocky peaks, gushing streams and waterfalls. All along the route the air was filled with the soothing rushes of wind and the muffled dash of valley-bound water.

Jewel Basin lies east and slightly north of Bigfork and approximately 17 miles from both Kalispell and Columbia Falls, straddling the Swan Range within sight of Flathead Lake to the west and Hungry Horse Reservoir to the east. It is a hiker's and backpacker's dream and has more than fulfilled what the Forest Service envisioned when giving the area its special designation a decade ago: No logging or other resource extraction is permitted in the

View from the trail to Jewel Basin. ROBERT GILDART

basin, nor are horses or other domestic livestock or motorized vehicles.

When the Jewel Basin Hiking Area was created the Forest Service had in mind an easily accessible place that contained a trail system conducive to short, family hikes. It was to offer people of all ages the opportunity to enjoy nature without the need for exotic equipment or great physical endurance. So far the area has discharged its duty well.

Easy access is the region's premier asset. Roads come near the boundary in both the Noisy Creek and Graves Creek drainages, on the west and east sides respectively. In addition to Graves Creek, the northern and eastern portions of the area are accessible along the West Side South Fork Road parallel to Hungry

Horse Reservoir via Wounded Buck Road. West Fork Clayton Creek and Clayton Access may also be gained on Krause Creek Road near the northeast corner of Jewel Basin.

Noisy Creek Road is by far the most popular access, used by 80 percent of the recreationists entering the area according to the Forest Service. It is within the closest walking distance to a lake in Jewel Basin. The road is rough and rocky and unsuitable for trailers, but passable for small passenger cars. It's only a stone's throw from Bigfork and the second closest access from Kalispell.

Once within the boundaries of Jewel Basin the hiker has at his disposal more than 15,000 acres of high mountain back country characterized by glacier-carved peaks and cirques that surround valleys dotted with 30 alpine lakes. Thirty-five miles of trails connect most of the lakes, and aside from getting from the valley floor to the basin rim, most of the hiking is not strenuous. The elevation, which varies from a low of 4,200 feet to 7,529 atop Mt. Aeneas, averages close to 6,000 feet above sea level.

Mountain goats are common, along with elk, mule deer and a few whitetail deer. Black bears, grizzlies and an occasional mountain lion are also known to live in the basin. Upland game birds like the Franklin grouse and blue grouse are in good supply, as are ruffed grouse. Fur-bearing animals in the region include pine martens, weasels and coyotes. There are also sparse populations of lynxes, minks, beavers and badgers.

Fishing in the basin's lakes is quite good and populations of westslope cutthroat trout in many of the lakes are maintained by the Montana Department of Fish, Wildlife and Parks through a planting program. Big Hawk, Birch, Black, Blackfoot, Wildcat, Pilgrim, Clayton and Crater Lakes are cited most often as providing the best fishing.

All manner of baits and lures have proven effective. Shiny brass lures and red spinners are sometimes called for, as are cheese, marshmallows and night crawlers. Flies, too, can be effective if the fish are rising near the shore or if one is exceptionally keen and long of cast with a fly rod. In my opinion, an enterprising and hardy party that managed to backpack in a small inflatable raft would undoubtedly find success in the deeper, center portions of the bigger lakes.

Lakes occupy 383 acres, about two percent of the total land area, in Jewel Basin. Clayton Lake in the northeast corner supports a cutthroat trout population. At 58 acres it is the basin's largest body of water, and at 100 feet nearly the deepest. Next in size come Upper Black Lake, Wildcat Lake and Birch Lake. The last, at 150' deep, is close to the Noisy Basin access and provides excellent fishing with its populations of rainbow and cutthroat trout.

Interest in preserving the unique status of the Jewel Basin area began in the 1950s when an infestation of spruce bark beetle caused logging activity to accelerate in the particular area of the Swan Range. A group called Flathead Wildlife, Inc., met with officials of the Swan Lake Ranger District to discuss the possibility of securing a wilderness classification for that portion of the range. Their original proposal outlined an area four miles wide and 50 miles long, stretching from Bad Rock Canyon south all the way to Swan Peak.

As negotiations progressed, both parties agreed that the area of greatest attraction along the range was the small section near Bigfork that contained the highest concentration of alpine lakes. One small cluster of three lakes in the area was called Jewel Basin—the name deemed appropriate to the surrounding terrain as well and ultimately adopted for what is now 15,349 acres of hiking area.

In 1958 the Montana Wildlife Federation endorsed a Wild Area proposal for the Jewel Basin, but according to the Forest Service document on the establishment of the hiking area, interest in this proposal was "generally dormant."

Another wildlife group, the Montana Wilderness Association, passed a resolution in 1962 urging the Forest Service to study the possibilities of creating a Wild Area in Jewel Basin, and later in the year the idea received support from Senator Lee Metcalf of Montana.

In 1963 the Forest Service conducted a study on the region and set the boundaries for the proposed Jewel Basin Wilderness Area, which encompassed what eventually became the hiking area.

The basin lost ground in its bid to become classed as wilderness in 1964 when Congress passed the Wilderness Act, a move that caused the proposal to be put aside while areas already designated as "primitive" were selected for first study for possible inclusion into the National Wilderness System.

Subsequently the area was designated for individual campground destinations. Most of the frequently-used campsites near popular lakes are within easy walking distance of discreet toilets. Trails are well maintained and, even during the runoff, erosion is minimized on steep slopes by trail improvements and additions that have buttressed the soil.

If Crater Lake is typical of the area, then Jewel Basin is indeed a gem. During the trip in, my son and I witnessed a constant parade of wildflowers, losing count after a dozen varieties, ranging from beargrass, Indian paintbrush and white and yellow lilies to tiny, delicate blue flowers resembling forget-me-nots.

The lake itself was cool and inviting as ever a mountain pond could be. The pure and lucid blue-green water allowed me to follow my lure from the instant it hit the water until the moment I retrieved it for another cast.

I hooked one small one after lunch and let him go. The rest of the afternoon, instead of showing appreciation for my act of mercy and sportsmanship, the fish taunted me. While the sun arced across the sky on its most northerly ecliptic, dim, gray shapes nosed lazily after my shiny lure in gestures of contempt. Or worse yet, took me to the height of frenzy by making headlong rushes at the spinner only to veer off sharply at the last instant.

Finally the mocking was too much to bear. Laying aside my pole I stripped and dived headlong into their pool, where I thrashed and frolicked, letting out great whoops of icy delight while I strove to violate as best I could the sanctity of their environment—a vain but wonderfully refreshing endeavor.

Late in the day a tingling, sunburned head and the rising of a waxing moon signalled the time to return to camp. Son David, also, was a luckless angler that day. We feasted mightily, though despondently, upon freeze-dried vegetarian stew on the longest day of the year.

That night Crater Lake, but one of many jewels in the crown, lulled me to sleep with the gentle slap-lapping of waves on the shore.

And to think I could be there any time, four hours after leaving Bigfork.

THE LOWER RIVER

Wagon Train—A Journey Through Time

"Move 'em out," hollared Wagon Master Forrest Davis to the line of covered wagons as he snapped the reins over the team of horses hitched to his own wagon. With that call more than a dozen wooden-wheeled wagons began to move from Pablo toward the distant hills that are a part of the Flathead Indian Reservation. The scene was one that could have occurred in Montana less than a century ago, particularly in this stretch along the Flathead River.

"We're trying to grasp some appreciation of the joys and hardships our parents experienced as they settled the area," said Davis. "An outing such as this does a pretty good job of showing us what life was like along the trail."

Indeed, as the wagon train progressed throughout the long spring day toward the first night's camp, its numbers increased. Behind Davis were now over 30 old-fashioned wagons that wound their way through prairie and badlands.

If appearances can be said to count for anything, this was a replica of the genuine wagon trains that had already traveled across much of the great west—bound everywhere, trying anything—to fulfill hopes and dreams in a land where nothing was thought impossible.

"Every year our trip is a challenge," said Davis. "Last year we had us a runaway. Another year a near drownin'. One year we had us a weddin' and a buryin' both on the same day. Something bound to happen this year too. Don't know what, but we've got over 65 miles of harsh, sagebrush-covered land to travel before we reach White Earth Creek. Unless it warms up, it'll be too cold for rattlers. And that's too bad. We've always had us a snake cook-out before."

For 16 years the West Montana Wagon Association has been traveling cross-country, cooking snakes, and increasing each year in popularity. Although the organization is a loose-knit one, it does hold annual meetings to discuss improvements and conditions. Anyone can join the group, although each must have a wagon that does not have rubber wheels. Guests are welcome, but must have a sponsor. This year more than 150 people converged from different directions—California, Oregon and Washington—but most were from Montana, particularly the farming areas of Flathead country.

By late afternoon, the group had reached Sloan's Bridge and made camp. Dogs were chained to wagon wheels so they wouldn't become "coyote bait." Dinner was hastily prepared; the "settlers" were anxious for the night's activities.

As dusk descended over the wagon train, those with a talent for music gathered around a campfire and began strumming their guitars, passing a bow across their fiddles, blowing into mouth harps or squeezing their accordions.

Two of the best-known in the group were Jeri and Craig Halford, who several years before had captured the imagination of the group. Along the route, they had been married. Side by side on two well groomed horses the couple had advanced to the wilderness altar for their wedding vows.

Jeri Halford is also well known as the president of the Polson Old-Time Fiddlers, a group that attempts to preserve music of the pioneer era. As the campfire crowd gathered, Jeri rosined her bow and deftly drew earthy chords that penetrated the night air and overpowered the murmur of the nearby river.

With his guitar, Craig joined in. Then he began a happy refrain. "Like a storybook ending I'm lost in your charms...Come waltz across Texas with me."

Others joined in—tapping their feet. Before long, a number of couples were kicking up sagebrush as they performed the two-step.

"The evening we were married," beamed Craig, "folks were playing the guitar for us. What a night we had! It was something like this, with every song imaginable being played..."

Nearby the river glistened from the moonlight shining over the shadowy backbone of the snow-capped Mission Mountain Peaks. Somewhere out in that great expanse, a lone coyote howled.

Morning comes early along the river. Birds chirped at the first light of dawn, but already aromas from bacon, potatoes, eggs and freshly-made coffee seeped through the camp. Among these folks there's a passle of early risers appearing almost exuberant to greet each new day.

One of the first significant landmarks the group passed is the Big Bend, located near the

Men, women, children—and a dog—try to discover something of the toils, hardships and pleasures experienced by their ancestors.
ROBERT GILDART PHOTOS

93

Riding and bouncing through exquisite country by day to hear the knee-slapping music of old-time fiddlers at night. ROBERT GILDART PHOTOS

Little Bitterroot River. This is the area where the Pablo-Allard bison herd was contained in the century's early years. Stock from this herd formed the nucleus of today's national bison herd that lives along the southern portion of Flathead country.

In earlier days, a drift fence crossed the "isthmus" of the Big Bend. It was thought the river and fence would contain the beasts. But the scheme failed. The animals didn't recognize the massive Flathead River as a boundary. The inevitable run and subsequent regrouping, repeated over several years, was later designated by newspapers as "The World's Largest Roundup."

Almost as high as the mountains comprising the Bison Range to the south is Grund's Hill. From the Hill, one can see McDonald Peak and McDonald Glacier in the background. Nearby is the Flathead River, rolling like a ball of blue flaxen yarn along an uneven surface.

In the spring, Grund's Hill is dotted by a multitude of colors. Within the hill's drier sites are found the crimson-flowered bitterroot, while areas that receive a modicum of moisture grow lupine, prairie smoke and arrow leaf balsamroot. It would be hard to imagine a more tranquil setting.

That thought must have been on the mind of one of the wagon train's former members. So lofty is the area that the man chose it as his final resting place. During the 1983 covered wagon trip, the man's ashes were scattered along the hill's steep slopes.

For all of its beauty, the hill has a reputation for being downright cantankerous. Considerable skill and alertness are needed by the wagon masters to negotiate the grade and avoid incurring the same mishaps that occurred in years gone by. One time, when the group was new and relatively inexperienced, a wagon broke loose and rolled over. The driver was pinned beneath, sustaining severe injuries for which he was later hospitalized.

Forrest Davis knows about the hazards of working around horses. In 1983, while he was clocking an Indian relay race in Polson, two horses collided. The force of the impact threw one of the animals high into the air and across the fence. That animal landed on top of the 61-year-old Davis, breaking his neck and crushing his pelvis. When Davis finally awoke from his week-long coma he was advised he might not walk again.

But now, out in front with his wagon and ready to begin the descent is Forrest Davis. Standing erect but leaning on the cane he must occasionally use when he grows tired, the onetime horse and mule tamer—still active as a horse trainer—surveys the group behind. Satisfied, Davis waves his hand forward and the group begins its descent.

Close behind is a burly bearded man named Carl, driving a heavy, two-mule-team wagon. Nestled beside him is his dog. With a pull on a lever, Carl brakes hard on the rear wheels and then starts down the precipitous trail. The wagon creeps forward, and the horses are content that the monster bearing down behind them is not gaining ground.

This year there will be no runaways. After several suspenseful hours, the long hill is negotiated. Just ahead is the evening's campsite, located amidst a grove of ponderosa trees that flank the Flathead River.

The next day is one that has been designated for layover. Many take the opportunity to saddle horses and strike out in different directions. Some ride for the crest of the tallest hill in the area, knowing that from this vantage they can catch a glimpse of the great lake 20 miles to the north.

Others ride down a trail that parallels the river toward an old homestead that has a wonderful history. The cabin and corrals are located where the river assumes a configuration resembling the shape of a horse shoe; hence the ride is across "Horse Shoe Bend."

The cabin, located toward the curved part of the shoe, is said to have been built by one who had been an advisor to Chief Joseph of the Nez Perce tribe. Not far from the cabin are a collapsed root cellar and an active osprey nest. In another direction are two graves—both of children. There are so many questions to spark

the imagination, and so little time to probe for answers.

Campfire settings always bring out the best of the imagination, in both serious and light-hearted veins. Around one campfire there is an intense silence followed by prolonged laughter. It's a night for tall tales, and one stocky man has the crowd entranced.

"Bulldog" is telling of a man with whom he'd placed a wager. Firelight pulsates off the face of the listeners, and the barrel-chested man concludes his story. More logs are added to the fire and restless sparks shoot upward.

"My father," says Ed Bratton, "used to chop ice from the Flathead to keep our produce cold. That, of course, was before electricity came to the Flathead somewhere in the '30s."

Another man tells of his father's adventures in Polson and of his coming into the country via Ellis Island. George Moore and his wife, who celebrated their 61st anniversary on the wagon train, recall their years as packers.

More time, and the darkness grows more steely. As it does, a great horned owl hoots to its young. The sounds are taken as a cue for most men, woman and their families to drift off. A few remain by the fire, waiting for the return of teenage children gone night riding to hear a den of coyote whelps yipping, yapping and yelping.

Next morning there was a vibrancy in the cool river air that affected horses, mules, dogs and people. Pop-eyed children stared at their surroundings while men shouted orders to one another. Nearby, dogs barked while horses and mules pawed the ground, quickly scraping out ruts in the earth beneath their iron-clad hooves.

Stepping into the seat of the covered wagon, Pete snapped the reins, signaling the two massive draft horses to move. With an almost premeditated determination, the two Belgians lurched forward. Then they veered right—and the wagon, loaded with cargo, driver and dog—bounced high over a log, tottered precariously for a moment and came to rest in a hard knot of juniper brush. Quickly the team was

Running Buffalo Rapids on the lower Flathead River.
ROBERT GILDART

quieted by anxious men moving in with deliberation. Unhitching, the men turned to extracting the wagon.

Forty-five minutes later the wagon had been pulled free. No damage had been sustained by the "singletree," harness or wagon. Soon, the team was back in its traces, ready for the last grind, a haul through the White Clay Cliffs and the fording of White Earth Creek.

"It's been a another good trip," pronounced wagon master Forrest Davis, relying on his cane once again to stand and stretch his game leg. "And I thank my lucky stars I'm healthy and well enough to be along and learn something new. Each trip we learn better how to cope with stubborn critters and, particularly, how to make things work together.

"And I think that was one of the most important aspects of our parents' experiences, this overcoming of hardships and the making of things work with family, friends and neighbors in this rough part of Flathead country."

Behind us now the endless windswept expanse of land had no audible response. The wind was subdued in the cloudless sky and the sun beamed down warmly. The land and river were satisfied for the moment to express themselves in terms of their restless, ever-changing, but now-quiet beauty.

PART IV

FUTURE OF THE FLATHEAD

AN ECOSYSTEM VIEW

Somers Bay on Flathead Lake. RAY MILLER

In the predawn gloom of August 19, 1986, Paul Stelter stood on Bird Point on the south shore of Flathead Lake, preparing to attempt an end-to-end swim of the lake. Although the feat had been attempted before, all the previous attempts had been aborted because the cold water had dropped the body temperatures of the swimmers and brought on hypothermia. Stelter hoped to avoid that problem with the aid of a special wetsuit designed for triathletes. At 6:00 a.m., he dived into the 68-degree water of Flathead Lake and began the 25-mile swim. Fifteen miles and about eight hours later, in the vicinity of Yellow Bay, he "felt I couldn't make it. But when I saw that sign, I knew I could do it." The sign, held by friends who had launched their boat to come out and encourage him, read "You can do it."

Just over 14 hours after diving into the water near Polson, Paul swam within sight of the crowd of 250 supporters who had gathered at Wayfarers State Park to cheer him on. Amid chants of "Go, Paul, go! Go, Paul, go!" he climbed stiffly onto the rocky shoreline, waved to the cheering crowd, and wrapped himself in a blanket.

In Stelter's words, he undertook the swim "first as a personal challenge, and secondly to promote an awareness of the lake and its quality."

While the lake itself was the focal point for Stelter's swim, it cannot be separated from the rest of Flathead country. The aquatic environment of the lake is strongly influenced by its entire 4.5-million-acre watershed. Natural events and human activities throughout the upper Flathead drainage add sediments, nutrients, ions and organic matter to the rivers, most of which are ultimately discharged into the lake. During an average year, Flathead Lake

Clockwise from top left:
Hydroplane racing. JAN WASSINK
Looking across Flathead Lake toward the Swan Range. TOM DIETRICH
Pleasure boat docks. RICK HULL
Trophy for a two-year-old. JAN WASSINK

97

Top: Prime Flathead Lake mackinaw. NEIL H. JENSEN
Above: Ice fishing on the lake. ROBERT GILDART
Right: The eternal beauty of Flathead Lake. ROBERT GILDART

receives a flow of 8.8 million acre-feet of water from its tributaries. Since the lake volume is 18.8 million acre-feet, or 2.1 times the annual inflow, almost half of the lake volume is replaced by river water each year. (See page 8.)

The challenge for saving Flathead Lake is similar to Stelter's. Assessment of the problem is near completion right now. More than 24 studies, conducted by five different groups and sponsored by nine agencies, are in progress. Other studies, already completed, have looked at most of the "important" aspects of the ecology of Flathead Lake. Flathead country is, without a doubt, one of the most intensively studied areas in the state.

These studies have highlighted many areas of concern, each affecting different people within Flathead country. Pollution is probably the first concern that comes to mind, and it will affect us all—from the swimmer who develops swimmer's itch, to the fisherman whose favor-ite trout waters support only suckers, to the lakeshore owner who can no longer drink the water, to the downtown businessman whose income is down because fewer tourists are interested in vacationing on a polluted lake. But, water fluctuations and water temperature changes due to the operation of Hungry Horse and Kerr dams also affect the lake. Soil erosion—resulting from road construction, poor logging practices, excessive livestock grazing, the elimination of streambank vegetation, irrigation returns and channelization—is also a problem. Development along the rivers and along the lakeshore, with the accompanying septic tanks, also has its effect. Proposals for new dams—the most recent would have inundated the wild water below Kerr Dam—seem to surface regularly as out-of-area demands for power increase. Proposals for oil, gas and mineral exploration are constantly under consideration for one part of Flathead country or another.

98

Even developments north of the border, in Canada, threaten Flathead Lake, as evidenced by the Sage Creek Coal company, a Canadian firm, which is proposing a coal mine on Cabin Creek, a small creek that empties into the North Fork of the Flathead River 12 miles north of the border.

Dr. Jack Stanford of the University of Montana Biological Station at Yellow Bay has analyzed core samples taken from the bottom of the lake. Stanford and his cohorts are able to look back into history to get an idea of the future. "Each year," says Stanford, "is separated by a thin layer of pollen—washed downstream or blown from trees flanking the lake. This pollen filters through the water and is deposited on top of last year's sediment. From this we can assess the amount of sedimentation that is created each year." Such measurements conducted by scientists indicate that drastic changes have taken place in the Flathead Lake system, particularly in the last 10 to 20 years.

In some areas, this increase in siltation has virtually eliminated trout reproduction. To hatch, trout eggs must be placed in water with relatively high oxygen content. Silt, by sifting into and filling the spaces between the gravel in spawning streams, reduces the oxygen available to the eggs and fry, and so reduces hatching and survival.

Stanford's research revealed that silt is not the only thing that is building up in Flathead Lake. Undesirable nutrients, such as phosphates and nitrates, are also on the increase. These chemicals originate from different sources—discharge of inadequately treated sewage from the valley's major communities, faulty or misplaced septic systems and agricultural runoff.

As a result of this increase in phosphorous, an unprecedented "bloom" of blue-green algae occurred in Flathead Lake in the summer of 1983, putting the general public on notice that changes were happening. The algae, and other plant growth resulting from the increase in available nutrients, die, settle to the bottom and decay, adding still more nutrients to the

Above, left and right: Researchers from the Yellow Bay Biological Station explore land and water. ROBERT GILDART

Left: Cattle pastured along the North Fork, north of Polebridge. TOM DIETRICH

99

water. At the same time, the water becomes more turbid, increasing the absorption of sunlight and thus increasing the water temperature, leading to still more plant growth, more nutrients, and higher water temperatures—a process called eutrophication.

Stanford's research has highlighted the problem and also pinpointed the solution. Only a small fraction of the phosphorous entering the lake is bioactive—in a form usable to the algae. About two percent of the lake's bioactive phosphorous can be attributed to agricultural runoff and forestry practices. The other 98 percent comes from domestic wastewater. One-fourth of that phosphorous comes from laundry detergents.

A movement to adopt an ordinance banning phosphate detergents from all of Flathead County likely will be passed into law in the very near future. Other sources of phosphorous pollution could be eliminated by upgrading existing sewer systems in Kalispell, Bigfork, Whitefish and Columbia Falls. Establishing systems in Lakeside, Somers and Evergreen would also help.

Most of the other threats to Flathead Lake also have been assessed. The technology to solve most of these problems is available. Cooperation is a question.

The necessary cooperation must come from the managing agencies, which, unfortunately, in Flathead country are a mish-mash of often-conflicting jurisdictions. Some of the organizations directly involved in the future of the Flathead's natural resources are the National Park Service, the federal Fish and Wildlife Service, the United States Department of Agriculture Forest Service, the Bonneville Power Administration, the Environmental Protection Agency, the Bureau of Reclamation, the Army Corps of Engineers, the Bureau of Indian Affairs, the federal Energy Regulatory Commission, Montana Power Company, the Montana Department of Fish, Wildlife and Parks, the Montana Department of Health, the Montana Forest, the Confederated Salish and Kootenai Tribes, the Flathead County govern-

Above: Hunting party along the South Fork of the Flathead. ED WOLFF

Right: Entrance to Yellow Bay Biological Station. TOM DIETRICH

ment, the Lake County government and the Canadian national government. Many others are indirectly involved. Out-of-basin interests also will have an influence on the resources by their insistent demands for the oil, gas, hydropower and water.

The agencies directly involved in the Flathead will be making a decision, either by action or inaction, on whether the Flathead ecosystem will be managed cooperatively as an ecological unit. Or, if each agency continues to support only its own special management interests, the result will be a fragmented approach to managing these vast natural resources.

It can, however, be done. A case in point is the kokanee salmon. Through the '60s, kokanee spawned prolifically along the shores of Flathead Lake and along the main stem of the Flathead River. In the mid '50s, biologists from Fish, Wildlife and Parks noticed that dropping water levels in the lake, as a result of Kerr Dam power production, often left redds high and dry. Exposed to the elements, the eggs either dried up or froze, killing the fry.

By the late '70s, the operation of Hungry Horse Dam also changed—to a power-peaking mode. This resulted in large discharges in the fall while the kokanee were spawning. In

winter, limited power production resulted in lower water levels in the river. Just as in Flathead Lake, redds were left high and dry. Between 1975 and 1985, the number of spawning kokanee in the main stem dropped from 100,000 to about 10,000.

In the early 1980s, the Northwest Power Act was passed, providing money to mitigate damage done to fish and wildlife habitat by the construction and operation of hydropower projects. This provided Fish, Wildlife and Parks with necessary funding to begin detailed studies on the problems of the kokanee. Those studies have already begun to bear fruit. Power production of Hungry Horse Dam was altered in 1982 to maintain sufficient levels of water in the river to keep the kokanee redds covered. As a result of this change, the number of spawners in the main stem is rising.

The cooperation needed to benefit the kokanee can also be achieved in respect to other problems. Commitment will be the key. The lake will be safe only when enough people feel as does Paul Stelter: "This is a precious thing we've got here, and we need to take care of it. And any way we can protect it, that's what we have to do."

Top left: Visitors at the Mt. Brown lookout above Lake McDonald. BRUCE SELYEM
Top right: Sailboats on Bigarm Bay near Wildhorse Island. RAY MILLER
Right: Canada goose fitted with radio collar. KRISTI DuBOIS

Overleaf: Hungry Horse Reservoir. ROBERT GILDART

Next in the Montana Geographic Series

Montana's Homestead Era
The homesteader was a pioneer in a wave of settlement that embodied much of the American dream: land to be had merely by "proving up." "Honyockers" or nesters, as they were called, were lured by the thousands by outrageous descriptions of what the Montana prairie would bear. In a few years, most would be defeated and gone, and the landscape would never be the same. Their story is part of the Montana lore, part of the state's character. Dan Vichorek, Montana Magazine columnist, has set out to capture the color, the promise and the heartbreak of that time—as much as possible through the stories of the living homesteaders themselves.

Montana's Rocky Mountain Front
If any single place in Montana epitomizes its character, it is the Rocky Mountain Front. This is the mountainous face of the Rockies south of Glacier Park, where they lift above the vast plain of the eastern two thirds of Montana. The elevations of its craggy peaks are not Montana's highest, but nowhere is the relief from valley bottom to pinnacle more dramatic. At the same time, it is historically significant—a western barrier to development from the east. Its Sun River game range is home to a nationally significant band of bighorn sheep, wolves may be making a comeback here, birds of prey haunt its miles of cliffs. Perhaps most notable is the fact that the front is the last place in the United States where the grizzly roams out of the mountains onto the prairie where it once was lord.

The Montana Geographic Series:

Volume 1: Montana's Mountain Ranges
Volume 2: Eastern Montana: A Portrait of the Land and the People
Volume 3: Montana Wildlife
Volume 4: Glacier Country: Montana's Glacier National Park
Volume 5: Western Montana: A Portrait of the Land and the People
Volume 6: Greater Yellowstone: The National Park and Adjacent Wild Lands
Volume 7: Beartooth Country: Montana's Absaroka-Beartooth Mountains
Volume 8: Montana's Missouri River
Volume 9: Montana's Explorers: The Pioneer Naturalists
Volume 10: Montana's Yellowstone River
Volume 11: Montana's Indians, Yesterday and Today
Volume 12: Montana's Continental Divide
Volume 13: Islands on the Prairie: The Mountain Ranges of Eastern Montana
Volume 14: Montana's Flathead Country

Each volume is $13.95 plus $1.25 for postage ($15.20 total)

Discounts are available through our
Montana Geographic Series Subscription.

Montana Magazine

The history, the wild back country, the people, the wildlife, the towns, the lifestyle, the travel—these things are Montana—unique among the states. Montana Magazine brings you the Montana story six times a year in a beautiful, long-lasting magazine. Its hallmark is full-page color photography of Montana from the peaks to the prairies.

Regularly Featured Departments

Weather
Geology
Hunting and Fishing
Outdoor Recreation
Humor
Personality
Dining Out

Montana Magazine
The Most Complete Guide to Enjoying Montana

$15/year - 6 issues
$27 for 2 years

Montana Magazine
Box 5630
Helena, Montana 59604

About Our Back Cover Photo
This photographic mosaic was compiled from Earth Resources Satellite Photo passes made from a height of 570 miles. It was pieced together in black and white and interpreted in color by Big Sky Magic, Larry Dodge, Owner. Commercial Color Adaptation © 1976 Big Sky Magic.

Front cover photographs
Clockwise from left:
Flathead Lake near Lakeside at sunrise, looking toward the Swan Range. Tom Dietrich
Floating the South Fork of the Flathead River. Robert Gildart
Babcock Creek in the Bob Marshall Wilderness, headwaters of the South Fork of the Flathead. Lawrence Dodge
Mt. Harding in the Mission Range. Ray Miller